Turtle Pictures

Camino del Sol
A Latina and Latino Literary Series

Turtle Pictures

Ray Gonzalez

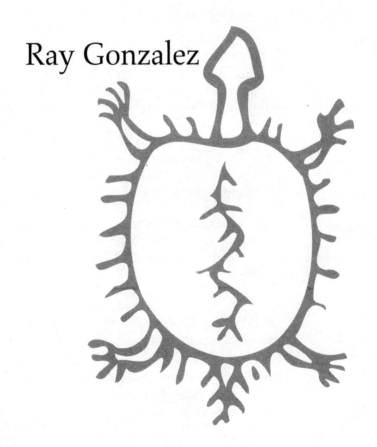

THE UNIVERSITY OF ARIZONA PRESS   TUCSON

The University of Arizona Press
© 2000 Ray Gonzalez
First Printing
All rights reserved

⊛ This book is printed on acid-free, archival-quality paper.
Manufactured in the United States of America

05   04   03   02   01   00   6   5   4   3   2   1
Library of Congress Cataloging-in-Publication Data
Gonzalez, Ray.
Turtle pictures / Ray Gonzalez.
p. cm. — (Camino del sol)
ISBN 0-8165-1964-1 (alk. paper)
ISBN 0-8165-1966-8 (pbk. : alk. paper)
1. Mexican Americans—Poetry. 2. Mexican Americans
—Civilization. 3. Turtles—Poetry. I. Title. II. Series.
PS3557.O476 T83   2000   99-6584
811'.54—dc21   CIP

British Library Cataloguing-in-Publication Data
A catalogue record for this book is available from the British Library.

Publication of this book is made possible in part by the proceeds of
a permanent endowment created with the assistance of a Challenge
Grant from the National Endowment for the Humanities,
a federal agency.

*"Formed by the minds of your ancestors,
the gods of your ancestors salute you."*

—*Patti Smith*

Contents

Acknowledgments

The author would like to thank the editors of the following publications where some of these pieces, often in earlier form, first appeared:

Bitter Oleander, Black Moon, LUNA, *Mid-America Review, New American Writing, Prairie Schooner, Quarter After Eight, Railroad Face (Chile Verde Press), Talking River Review, Terra Nova, Yefief.*

•

Names and Echoes, without whom this book would not be possible: Juan Felipe Herrera, Mark Turcotte, Diego Rivera, Patti Hartmann, Fernando Pessoa, Virgil Suarez, Ida Steven, Eduardo Galeano, John Bradley, Rudolfo Anaya, Paul Roth, Gary Snyder.

First Shell

He lived to be the other, contrary to the tracks of the turtles in the mud. He lived to follow the slow trail toward boundaries, fresh movements inside the earth — turtle missives given to him ages ago, granted the extension of a species that would come out of the sea and inhabit the great northern deserts without anyone in his family seeing how the secret turtle movements would possess them, retake them, shape them into the assimilated sleep of humans and creatures — startling evidence that the slow crawl and the peaceful harp of the turtles kept him alive, gave him a terrible loss, and made him move across the great landscapes he tried to shake off at birth.

◆

Hidden inside the wrist of a thief
Found embedded in the fingernail of a Mayan statue
Caught in the history of breathing
Turtle pictures framed between the great walls of stone
Turtle pictures moving to make way for the heart

Turtle pictures where everyone gets lost
Turtle frames where no one knows
Turtle ideas where the green surface of a cloud is the bestowed oven of the
    mind

◆

The Shell

When Cortez burned Mexico City, the stars glittered black in the sky before
the centuries of white light, four million birds scorched in the Aztec aviaries,
the conquistadores laughing as their torches set the moon of feathers on fire,
the stench turning the lake into the next world, clouds of amber calling to
    the birds to come alive centuries later, rolling across the lakes as if water
    could rise on its own without wings, without the centuries of white light
    touching anything that flies.

When Cortez burned Mexico City, brown faces came out of the water, fled naked
toward the heart that was never sacrificed, four million birds falling into
    great mounds of breathing earth, taking their time vanishing from the
    earth.

When I burned the house of my father, the color red turned brown and gave
    me time to come back. When I burned the house of my father, there was
    no one there.
No one knew I was there.

When the fires burned, the turtles survived—their gleaming hardness
    rolling into a mound
of several hundred turtles crawling over each other, trying to spit water into
    the flames,
moving toward the edge of the earth in order to attack the rays of sunlight
    penetrating the garlic trees,
the other survivors of the great change.

◆

Cocorima

the first street belongs to you.
it is paved with asphalt and the blood of old men

the first street walks toward you
it is narrow and cracked, breaking open to let you in
the first street has no name
it knows you and flows both ways
the first street found you without any shoes
it will wait for you to find your feet

the message is a blinding light
the message says the country is waiting for you
the message is painted on the back of the turtle

the words were plucked from the mouth of a young boy who did not know
    what he was saying—what had to be said so the hands of the maker
    could shape his life

Cocorima was installed behind his ear
Cocorima vibrating with unplugged guitars
Cocorima over the left shoulder
Cocorima answering the turtle prayers of men
Cocorima wanting to know how long it has to breathe
Cocorima inventing sorrow
Cocorima wanting to crawl into the steady heart
Cocorima stepping on the saxophone dropped by a cicada
Cocorima missing the threaded ice of a worshipped mouth
Cocorima insisting the captured ear belongs to the fields of corn

•

The man stepped on something limp. It set off an energy that grew into a di-
lemma, had no witness when I came down to see it. This fissure in his life was
bread, the apple left in his bag, a wife who loved him without cause, his way of
reading the broken twigs among the mint scented tree tops. The man opened
his wallet to find money glued to his photo, sweat on the seat of his pants re-
minding him how far he walked, the coins he dropped when he paused to see

if the fountain would rise for him. He seldom dreamed of moonless pilings embedded on the shore, rarely woke among broken sea shells carried farther than the canoe he lost long ago. There were strange tracks in the sand.

I walked with him before he was able to see, years before he could tell me the limited names for the water that wet our pants, mud washing too many ideas out of the rocks. We never reached the bay where he was born. He showed me where the blinding curve of beach collapsed toward where his house should have been. The man I learned from labored to find his breath, sent a letter to me before finding someone else's terror, another country that would take him and make him king.

"Do not step into the funny sky," he wrote. "Always bring your wife a piñon seed and a gift. Leave your bed unmade, so the mosquito knows the sun, and your stepson can lie back and watch TV. Don't remember me. The words I scribbled came out as strange sounds, the women of the past and a cry for something I can't mourn. Don't learn from me. If you imitate, it is not me, only the hands that bewilder you, rhymes that won't leave. The ocotillo limbs I gave you will drop their dry thorns into your attic trunk."

Before he disappeared, the man who invited me ate from the fruit of the saguaro, hoping I would quit following him. He showed me how easy it is to be betrayed by those who teach of the open boat and the swallowed sparrow wing, who swear by the word "shoe" and the cold lyric of dumbfounded men. The man wouldn't talk to me as he led me across the stream where we found the bleached leg bone of a cow. It was the place where tiny yellow apples fell from trees hundreds of miles inside the Gila wilderness, hours from the nearest road where he last spoke his poem, indistinguishable from the white haired chests of men.

•

All I saw was the river.
The brown faces coming out of the water.

All I saw was the river.
My father standing on the other side.

All I saw was the river.
The mountains slapping the sun without a place to hide.

All I saw was the river.
My mother's hands dripping mud, trying to hold up the walls.

All I saw was the river.
Young boys running to take over the bridge.

All I saw was the river.
Young girls opening their legs to change the course and the tide.

All I saw was the river.
The *brujo* stealing the moon and giving it to me to lick and bite.

All I saw was the river.
Voices calling me to go north and hide.

All I saw was the river.
Cesar Chavez not wanting anyone to make a movie of his life.

All I saw was the river.
Allen Ginsberg taking forever to get to the other side.

All I saw was the river.
My grandfather wanting more years to drink.

All I saw was the river.
Pancho Villa's horses galloping and exploding in the streets.

All I saw was the river.
My father's mother dying when he was five years old.

All I saw was the river.
I thought I was gone but the mud kept my shoes.

All I saw was the river.
James Wright slapping me until I wrote my first poem.

All I saw was the river.
Kenneth Rexroth cutting the desert with his sword of light.

All I saw was the river.
John Lennon stealing my Beatles vinyl 45s out of my mother's attic.

All I saw was the river.
The cactus cut into my imagination and made me leave.

All I saw was the river.
There is something I'm not saying here.

All I saw was the river.
Border Patrol cars surrounding the crowd.

All I saw was the river.
The drowned child floating across international boundary lines.

All I saw was the river.
Radioactive slime feeding millions and buying them more time.

All I saw was the river.
Río Grande Río Puerto Río de las Palmas moving inside my thumb.

All I saw was the river.
I crossed when there was nothing to cross and haven't crossed since.

All I saw was the river.
The sun brings back the brown faces.

All I saw was the river.
My grandmother spun me through the air when I was one year old.

All I saw was the river.
The mud brings back the brown faces.

All I saw was the river.
Water opened my eyes and water fed me until I cried.

◆

When the tired masker bestows hands and shells and the fasting prayer, you must listen to what he has to say. He has been doing this for centuries and knows the next millennium will be flying toward his dream of the rivers and towns that resisted mud and became mud. When the tired masker insists on lighting a fire, smell the air before you breathe the smoke. When the tired masker takes your hand, recall the shield painted on your back by your lover. It is large, green, blue, with moving, boiling centers of skin that the tired masker wants to take for himself. When it rains and tiny creatures crawl toward his home, he has already plundered their minds for the energy of the next century. It has to do with heartbreaks that injure huge beasts. It belongs to the child's eyes respecting the horizon. It has to do with wanting to tell the real story, the long sought tale of the woman with white hair and the man with white hair, two white haired turtles demanding power, with lifetimes of nothing but silence.

◆

Frame for a Tired Painting (1)

Asking for the relief of a spinal dance
Waiting for the train to resemble green arrows erasing the earth
Crying as if the coyote never came to sharpen its teeth
Sleeping under the warm embers of the volcanic arm
Waking before the sun suspends the mountain and retreats
Playing house with skeleton chambers of a family who fled a thousand years
    ago

Imagine you are sitting in a world full of turtles
You don't know what they are
They came out of your hair and made your grandmother a liar
They hiss only to themselves and surround you with love
If you could say the right thing they would disappear
The earth would finally understand its sister if they became extinct
Strength would be gained by all of this
Imagine you are sitting in a world full of turtles
You have always known what they are:

Limits.
Vocabulary.
Claws.
Boundaries.
Visitations.
Manners.
Eyes.
Tracks.
Limits.

Vocabulary.
Bleeding drums.
Sweat.

Computerized feet.
Claws.
Boundaries.
Departures.
Aggression.
Manners.
Hands.
Signs.
Limits.

◆

Finally getting to the point of having to define what it is.
Moving to the dance of announcing the first turtle was white.

Not caring if the second appeared green.
Always accepting the river came this way in abundance.

Home as a story.
As a theory.

Belonging in the palm where all things are told.
Sacrifice.

Willing to invent a version that will not frighten anyone away.
The continent has not been notified of the galaxy.

◆

San Jacinto Plaza, 1960

The fountain in the plaza cascaded dirty water, rose above the crowd watching
five alligators trapped there. They moved heavily toward the trash and food

thrown at them, one or two crunching coke cans, no one from the city keeping the tormentors away. They found one dead alligator with three arrows in its neck, finally sent the rest to the zoo. Downtown El Paso lost its monsters, replaced by hookers hanging around the bus stops when I walked by as a boy. I searched for something to replace the alligators, waited for the plaza to become a miniature Christmas village. The tall tree ignited in white and blue lights the night my parents took me to see Santa. I realized there was no such thing as St. Nick when the guy in the suit called the little girl ahead of me a crybaby, his impatience disappearing as I stared, thousands of lights and Christmas villages blinking into a city, the fountain frozen as the look on that Santa who noticed I knew what he was. I skipped my turn on his lap to find the alligators in the pool waiting for me to hang over the railing so they could respond to my movement, slap the water with their long, heavy tails so lights couldn't settle onto their moving mouths.

◆

When you look down, the slow memory of something crawling toward the
    truth
invents itself with the diamonds, circles, and rings of a green birth.

The hiss is the mother calling to the island that became a desert unable to sit in the palm of her hand.

The head retracts into the shell and spills a lost thought about how the
    ground
belongs to items listed inside a bead worn around the neck of the hunter.

This has something to do with moving mouths.

◆

Frame for a Tired Painting (2)

Read this:

I was alone when I woke and the truth had already started pouring out of my head. It was long ago, when I was still a child and the desert was enormous, without streets or houses, or schools, or freeways—the way the heart has been enormous and able to convert the stillness of the distance into the towering arms of my need. I was alone when I woke, but I knew it was the place I had to be, so I could find reason to behave and let the force of the isolated world touch its own boundaries and give me a chance to live. I had no idea for years. I had no way of knowing the pictures that kept falling out of me were signs to the passage where it disappeared.

◆

The boy had seen the traffic in the distance. He knew it was coming for him. He hid in the arroyo and loved the rocks and sand. He wrote poems for the tired walls and never gave in. The boy had seen the stars dread themselves by going out. He was not afraid. There was something else there with him. He knew it. He could feel it moving under the ground. He waited for it to emerge.

◆

The owl and the panther are trying to interrupt.
The owl and the panther want part of this.
The owl and the panther are trying to interrupt.

◆

Ponder this:

When the trumpet played, it was a barefoot jazz musician coming to stare at
   the water.

There was something swimming in the green haze.
When he touched the cold mouthpiece with his lips, he heard a splash.

From the terrace of the factory, he contemplated his retina.
From the running remains of a gift, he knew he had emerged from the sea.

♦

He wrote this upon seeing how the white terrain grew closer to his eyes:

no light but the search for you
  without lyrical panic
hunted inside readiness
    missing static
strum inside the waiting blood
  bestowed upon thieves
asking for news of singing bodies
no light but the search for you
  with night alone
hopeful stars looking for their beds
tunnels of whispers burrowing
  for a political hat
    letting go
inside the tongue
  bellybutton coffins humming inside
sticks fastened to the hair
  of a noticed man
    lifting his face to a point
taken for granted
  straw windows knotting their ideas
    toward fulfillment
impressed upon abundance
  no light but the search for you
    asking large ears to listen for hairs

as the square colors of music give up
       step on themselves for attention
wanting to be free as bare backs
              speaking to the earthquake
to stop speaking to the lateness of tomorrow
       under the drunk armpits of a god
chattering teeth forming new countries
         from the pregnant sky that throws up
     entrances and exits
no light but the search for you
         repeated to remind the throne to let go
     to be what it once was
before water dried into patterns that spelled

                         ♦

Phase for the red turtle that suddenly appears, lucid and long.

(Note found after the first extinction of the species, before its reinvention.)

I'll know the fog when the men who play with it
come back to strike me.

I'll sense the word when the face of another
catches me as I fall.

I'll respect the cruel thigh brandishing requests
upon my lifted body.

I'll answer the glass beetle and remain faithful
to the idea of rice and some kind of milk.

I'll dispose of tired streetlamps and build
a history of involvement and the tainted shoe.

I'll catch the bitter downpour and leave
two towns without having been gone.

I'll whisper the first notes and subtract
the cut healing in my palm.

I'll close my imagination with two lumps of coal
and feel for heat that was never there.

I'll slip beside the trapped oblivion and wonder
what I was talking about.

I'll explain the confession on a thin piece of paper
lie down to sleep on each word.

◆

I pass through time and fountains of madmen following me. They have fallen
off the cliffs because they do not understand what I am trying to say. They
think the turtle meat was the only thing I wanted. They saved the scorched
shells and wore them around their necks. There is no gift in this. I pass through
time and fountains of judges surround me. They know the island has spread
into this desert and we can't go back. They do not want me to talk about things
that do not exist. They ate long ago and have hated me for years. They pre-
fer the lizard and the snake, don't see why I have been slow in following the
slower turtles, when all I have to do is leap and open my eyes.

◆

After Effects

So there are tickets
    I have grown as flowers,

falling early despite my tongue.
I can't find the situation:
      the narrow color of a bed
filled with restless crimes.

So there are bees
      in the chapter on love,
failing to buzz despite passion.
                 I saw the mole on her back:
      an eye for the lonely dance
traced with fingers alone.

So there is magic in departure
      instead of confusion,
basking on time inside pomegranate
windows replaced with shade:
      the evening flees on a wooden table
where I carved my name and sighed.

So there are places hidden
      in the breast unkissed,
asking to be a pair of storms
abandoning romance for signs:
      one mouth is fascinating and asks that
I give it a second chance at love.

                        ♦

I no longer wait for the sun. It comes up on its own. I forgot the axis of cotton-woods this year. I was busy searching for the fists of color bursting inside my hands. I wanted testimony and gave up on the sun, wanted someone to tell me why I took the wheel of trust apart, set it in the fields of rain that dried years ago. Quiet things obey me. I compose sentences from the folding wings of dying butterflies, thoughts that embarrass me when I could say more, but I no longer step under the darkened thighs of trees. People come to me on their own. They want me to give them a word or two on how to sidestep their grief, enclose their hallucinations into words that lift them into a life yearned for by fools and poets who whisper, "There are no secrets in the exhausted loins of those who cry." I breathe for tomorrow, see an eagle talon embedded in the grave of my grandfather, his empty bottles of tequila disintegrating into the fields of rain whose broken glass bounces water into the faces of the few willing to walk with me. I send them away. They don't know how to envy the mud shivering down their backs. They won't enter the empty mission whose bell won't ring, can't recite from the forehead and call it an oath, nor admit they have another year without sacrifice.

◆

Tail

The story is out.

Once you were sustenance in the hand,
rich in the soil,
calling into the ground to retrieve water.

Lamentation.
Described to be found without the fear of the century's end.

Once you spoke to the echo,
traced its need for a signal to enter,
disturb what knelt behind a star
as if a star was a light that had no way
of knowing it was false.

Running to the active import,
extorted eye sold for love.
Fastened to the river by salt.

You were the failed wind,
but the wind changed to rain
and you reshaped your feet into claws,
sharp angels casting their flight toward
what burns, what talks back.

The story belongs in consequence.
Held back for the lover's shadow.
When it stops, it speaks.

It was your fingertip found
in a charcoal sketch inside a cave,
as if leaving the millennium was
the way to gain speed against the story
of the bellybutton, the muted jaw,
the arched back sweating against
windows opening onto a fault of flowers.

The room shudders inside short happenings—
their turn is protected by the power of singing.
Not one solid hand is called, consistent with greed.

Once you were that and gave nothing back,
tore your faith into bread beside cold ovens,
circled your mysteries with the sound of water,
invented a visitor who staggered you as a child,
telling your secret to the four directions,
so no bird could land on you,
mistake you for a smoldering piece of paper.

Smoking beside the plot of work.
The story is part of the moon, examined by each survivor.

First Shell

First the thorn, then the broken thorn.
The green head that prays and sees:
this is the end, the path where dust begins,
whether the mole tunneled through time or changed
the moment of its extinction.

When the water recedes, the green head watches—
another twin storm beside the body without end.

Capsule yellow with history.
Greedy cats entombed in the chest.
Fastened to a thumbnail sketch of anger and power.
You are still here performing tasks.

*Brought into reality with startled consequence—ask each man if he holds the
chair and listens for the favorite body to sit within it and confess how easily
it becomes a measure of his own desire—horn lust trailing the far green figure
as if bringing it back would secure a place in the hall of too much asking, too
many times hidden in the well.*

Vested stables judged by their own desire—
when the muscle recedes, there is a thin man sitting on the ground.
Frequent attacks of memory deny there is rapture—
twisted parlors become closets for the last man who stood up.

*The story is in.
It is over without reason—captured dimension implied and planted.
You are here somewhere, being kind and thoughtful.
A hair falls out of your head.*

Kindness offered to the saxophone before it became an endangered species.
How often it was seen on the corner brandishing its own temple.
The story is in.

When it was one lover, it was actually two.
When the elegant country no longer existed, the tale was lost.

◆

In the moment of the window, we are reminded we have not strayed far. We are still here, trying to discover why we are surrounded by large, desert turtles, their first emergence changing the day—their silence and petrified stance between tumbleweeds calling us to listen for the fireworks that celebrate the emptiness of the parking lot. In the moment of the window, feed yourselves and watch. The absent hands have a certain range. They know how to touch the revival and make it dance. The absent hands know the shell is the same rising alphabet found on the walls of the arroyo. In the moment of the window, the flugelhorn sounds like a weeping girl wanting to be rescued. Over the shrill echoes, a woman leans into the mud. Over the answering silence, a man is able to approach and love. The image is a pale shape and requires eggs laid in the mud. The image is the lost horse retracing the trail back to the wall. The image is a dirty alley full of garbage cans, rotten meat, and the flies that swarm and sing. The image is a man who can't be found across the tobacco fields, lost in cottonfields, instead, stepping into jalapeño fields that are more familiar to his bare feet, dreaming he could get lost in the orange groves, not knowing the huge nest of the wasps will fall on his head the instant he sets foot in America. He is thinking of the vato who sought peace, but found only bones in the street. He is recalling how one brilliant fool wired the neighborhood with hidden microphones, placing them in garbage cans, under rusting cars, right on telephone poles, and taped the sounds of the street, finding many conversations had nothing to do with him, whispers and cries and plots varnished by the young boys with shaved heads. This guy wore a T-shirt with a red turtle on the chest. He must have come from some other image, mistakenly placed here to remind us how the trail gets warmer as it grows by miles and miles and streets and handclaps.

◆

To the man hoping the mask falls off:
Look at your fingers, they are closed and important.

To the man hoping the mask is too tight:
Here is the love and the shining street.

To the man triangular as a gorging shark:
Here is the blood and the invitation to another world.

To the man asking for a chain of cardboard:
Look at how easily you forget the message.

To the man swallowing a whole cucumber:
There is room for a breathing stomach.

To the man understanding how ants march in a line:
You left something inside the finished music.

To the man thinking there were always two worlds:
Look at how quickly your hair has turned white.

To the man blowing his flugelhorn:
Listen to how many questions you have just asked.

To the man saying something out of despair:
Here is the sound of what you never had.

To the man facing the river before it floods:
Look at the kneeling man and how he finally moves.

◆

Biological assumptions:

When we move, the glands in the throat originate a liquid that is richer than the gold nailed to the first-born liver. The internal junction of blood and strength decides which form we take when we bow down and take apart the bones, the arteries, the canyon of skin we inherited from our fathers. Whenever we move the heart clogs up with the mistaken jelly of what we ate years ago, a continuous slab of stubborn sinew, a fusion of life and the dark energy castrated from a creature we never were, a three-legged prince who had too much love, too much sex, too many women coming to stare at his warped eye, how it heaved and sighed, how it wrote its name upon their naked backs, how his desire faltered like the soft touch of the tongue. Whenever we move, the arms and legs are shaved. They glisten and shine like the last picture we saw of the beautiful scarf, the harness of moonlit bodies touched with confession— the will to learn how to love again, a spouse who gave us love before she sailed on, the peacock who thought it was a crow, the crow who fed in the grass, pecked and gathered the last traces of our shed skin, flew away to build a nest out of bodies that never frightened it. When fear left us all, the crow turned into the frog tossed by boys into the air, hurled higher than the tallest tree, until the air turned green with the anger they never should have been fed— rain that covered their heads and taught them to jump farther than the nearest sound of those coming out of their houses in the dark to search for them.

The only touch in the room
firelight
was made

given to his mind
in frames holding ideas
of stone women in awe

up from the flesh
spoken of itself
drawn as art

on naked backs
crude figures
chewing

what they wanted
a life with motion
and charcoal

they gave him
weather and debt
sometimes their bodies

asking for replies
that say
fortune comes

from greed spilled
between the legs
of amber

how he took his time
with the intention
of roses

mistaking scent for love
asking dangling fires
to stop

smoke themselves
out of existence
caliber of lips

embraces
returning him
without a chance

to greet whatever
his fingertips
touched

◆

Come closer. You are a dense fabric. You belong with me because I am search-
ing for what was left behind—canyons and arroyos were too much and con-
fused me. I must stop and hear you speak. If you utter the right sounds, we can
define the dying century and be able to go on. If you say the wrong things, we
will be stranded here and have to eat the turds of the sun to be able to survive
and be given the maps that were regurgitated by flying reptiles. It sounds like
the wrong thing to compose, but you are standing here and my nerves have
begun to play the keyboards of the rock organ that has strange carvings on it.
Perhaps, those are the only words that need to hear the oral rope of calibers
and energetic confusions.

◆

I learned to shout above the wall,
followed my shadow into the adobe process.

I dried the mud on my face and chest,
learned to whisper through the corners of rooms.

I spoke between the lines of spiderwebs,
tasted the earth and it was handed to me.

I crunched pieces of dirt in my teeth without telling the wall.
I learned to find the cracks before they appeared,

followed my tongue over the smooth plaster.
I caused the room to get larger by cutting a window,

spoke to the sunlight as it came in and cleaned things.
I learned how to leave the clay alone and not swallow,

then called out to people, but they were only mud and straw.
I followed myself out through a man size hole in the wall.

◆

Get the fetish to do something.
Get it to arrive with the correct message.

◆

I saved the sacred mountain
by drinking a glass of Kool-Aid
when I was a boy.

◆

A taste of desire
cautions the brain.
A taste of desire
and there is no brain.

◆

All rivers rotate against the darkness.

◆

One voice sits down to eat.
Two voices devour the meal.

•

I enter the walls
sixty miles
west of my body.

Eight carved men
stick out
of the mud.

Two ovens lie
black
and closed.

I enter the walls
and believe
I am there.

A squirrel pelt hangs
from a tree
inside the room.

Sixty-two miles
west of my body
I am stopped
by a bowl of water.

The great house
of Saint Augustine
crumbles in
the sandstorm.

The great body
of Saint Augustine
sits in the graveyard
singing eighty miles
west of my body.

♦

Habitation

small day lying down on the floor—
trying to climb into a box—to do the walk inside the box—
to hear the train derailing—to start the shouting inside a flag—

to smear colors on the border of the mind—to face the hole
without knowing the hole faces you—to find its presence
inside the soul stepped on by an old dog—to move beyond question

and avoid each raindrop imposed upon your head—to finish flying
with a walk—to get the fetish to do something—to get it to arrive
on time—to leave imprints in the sand—to suit the sound of trouble

with lakes, birds—to blind the skin with worry—
to feed the flask with a missing arm—to light the notion with courage—
to agonize documents and ignore history—to hold a crown of concern

without letting it go—to fondle the bare stick and kiss it—to leave—
to swim inside a glass of history—to lie down on the floor and breathe—
to swell without reason—to be pure and love instinct—to sit the horse
    down—

to describe the feathers as repeating sounds—to comply with the wolf—to
    cry

as if crying was the wolf—to climb the stair and touch yellow ceilings—
to drink from bottles the way the heart drinks from the cross—to shudder

as a happy child—to trace a new tongue with the eye of a fish—to smell
the river before the current stands up—to smell the river before the mud
lies down—to smell the river before the bridge spans a third bank—

to turn around between folded hands—to put one hand on a dying swan—
    to watch
a mountain become a buried father—to hold the second hand before the
    heart—to dig
into the chest with nickels—to recover consolation and plant it in the
    cottonwood

to flee wisdom and bite it—to favor today buried in ice—to stand the
    invisible and stand
what is there—to catch balls of white gum as they fall out of the willow—to
    admit this is
the breath headed for the belly without the stomach for silence

◆

> *There are poets who service church*
> *clocks*
> >   —*Charles Simic*

The mountain in my hands belongs to people who worship mountains. I fell
down one long ago and have worn sunglasses ever since. The peak that de-
stroys my ability to write with my hands is used to the Band-Aid I wear on
one finger. It helps me trace the path of the river on the map. When I fol-
low the line, it is yesterday and no one has invaded yet. The conquest is still
a couple of hundred years away. I can't afford a cell phone, but know where I
am at all times. The mountain brings its own rain. I can predict how often it
showers and how many times the sparrow hawk is going to be poisoned. When

they found the latest carvings in the canyon, I was already there correcting the spelling. I defaced the ancient conversation because it was my mountain and no one could preserve it without making me stay stuck in the century of scientific inquiry. It is too much. I don't want to grow old with this mountain in my hands. There is greater potential in grasping the arroyo and digging for the fossils I left there thousands of years ago. After all, bone and shell never lie. They just fit nicely on my ring finger.

◆

I didn't let you in on the secret of the heat in the mattress, the morning of the virgin becoming the dawn of the first born, a day of dead senses beginning to perceive the world as it made light for the afterbirth, accessible buds of eagerness rising out of the mother to clean the room of the bed of coals kept burning for the man who wished his morning of birth had been postponed for years.

◆

The Turtle Christ

He came out of the water and looked at me. There was a glow I recognized as heaven, but I knew the earth was mud and had nothing to do with his light. I stared at him and his claws moved in the wetness without inching his body forward. I did not know what to do, so I stared and avoided his blessing. His great jaws opened and he hissed like the whole world was dying. I blinked my eyes and the glow finally came. He moved closer for the first time and I was frightened, not wanting to remember him as someone who was going to harm me in my days of asking and believing. The turtle Christ loved me by leaving something wet and putrid in the sand. Suddenly, he disappeared in the air and I thought I must be crazy. I stepped forward and looked down at the ground. The thing he threw up was an old, black beaded rosary whose smoothness shone and rose through the bubbles of mud.

◆

There are three words—*condition, avocado, bestow.*
They mean a clean table, a flat world,
the clown coming out of the blood to fry his worms
inside the canyon of time and disturbed thoughts.
They will be found inside the book and let go.
There are three words—*condition, avocado, bestow.*

There are two figures—*grandfather, headless statue.*
They describe the old world before it was conquered
by young men painting their chests to resemble women.
Grandfather with the whiskers of an ailing heart.
Headless man of ivory bending his knees to find the heart.
They will be found to have given the boy his beard.
There are two figures—*grandfather, headless statue.*

There is one filament—*electric line fusing the dream.*
It comes from the west and vanishes in the eye.
It accompanies the lonely man until he can't see.
It holds him back and teaches him to speak alone.
It glows with wisdom and fires knowledge into his chest.
It comes from the worm before it is stepped on by the old man.
It will secure its place in the bellybutton of the young.
There is one filament—*electric line fusing the dream.*

◆

As if some bird was recognized
in the frame of shadows
rending the tears

mistaking it for wings
shattered from gold desires
driven to imagine

how the king's chair
tore at the moment of
ecstasy

as if some hand developed
its own wisdom
reaching out

to carry the books
into the cold cells
before time

became a century
driven by armies
lost in blood

as a mistaken bird
survives the battle
without flying away

◆

The Province of Arroyo

When the earth opened, something came to me.
I listened against the mud walls and sighed.
When the earth removed its power,
I saw the blades of recognition come out of the ground,
conditions of desire mourning inside the rocks.
When the ground exploded in a rain of fossils,
I was no longer afraid.
I walked between the arms of heaven, saw it was only mud.

◆

Bent over the border, the shaman steals the moon.
Twisted over the river, the illegal alien drowns and dreams.
Flying into the house, the candles devour faith and reason.
Extended through the arms, the rosaries bind the body.

This is how the country begins
its way to the bare mountain,
petals of blooming cactus cutting faces on walls,
thorns glistening with white stars pulled
out of the jowls of brown faced men.
This is how the dirt road summons the jackrabbit, the roadrunner,
the rattlesnake cut into eighteen pieces by a grinning child.

This is the way to the drowning river,
the legs of the iguana turning red on the plate,
its three foot skeleton smelling like the river never ended,
water forming jail cells of silt breaking into the throats
of those who never made it across.

Bent over the border, no one screams in time.
Twisted over the barbed wire fence, the last person stains
the horizon with a silent scream that does nothing.

◆

The turtles are found inside the human body
They travel there searching for ice cream
crying to the wind to enlarge the stomachs of men
hissing to themselves to be patient and swim

The turtles are found inside the human body
They comb their hair and study the heart
sleeping in the intestines to nourish the search
waking in the bowels of a dream and flying out

First Shell

•

Once you were sustenance in the hand.
You were rich in the soil,
calling into the soil to retrieve water.

Once you were speaking to the echo,
tracing its need for a signal to enter,
disturb what knelt behind a star
as if a star was the light of dreams
that had no way of knowing they were false.

Once you were the failed wind,
but the wind changed to rain and you saw,
took your time reshaping your feet into claws,
sharp angels casting their flight toward
what burns, what talks back.

Once you were the fingertip found
in a charcoal sketch inside a cave,
as if leaving your millennium was
the way to gain speed against the story
of the bellybutton, the muted jaw,
the arched back sweating against
windows that opened onto a fault of flowers.

Once you were this and gave nothing back,
tore your faith into bread beside cold ovens,
circled your mysteries with the sound of water,
inventing a visitor who staggered you as a child,
telling your secret to the four directions,
so no bird could land on you and
mistake you for a burning piece of paper.

◆

Ten Horizons

1

The music in this long trance has value when the flowers take hold of my arms and scratch my skin with sorrow. When the teacher and the master marry each other, they recite fresh sayings from the livers of coyotes, don't bother to chew them as they swallow.

It is that obsession with taking in, taking out, taking hold, trying to keep the answer within the tumbleweed that refuses to cross the river as the wind loves it and cherishes its trail. It is too late to get closer.

The birthday. The celebration. The markings on paper calendars for friends, wives, those who close the dates around the years of getting older together. It is too late to get closer. The birthday.

The climb toward the sweetness of another time when I could enjoy the secret between words and not have to try to figure out what they meant without invoking the past mistakes of long dead ancestors who had to destroy me so they could die in peace.

It is too late to display. It is too late to go back. It is too late to convince myself I have not gotten there. There is still the chain of the locked image and the swollen fingers climbing into themselves without regret or the talent

to completely retell the story, trying to gain whatever salvation they have so they can negotiate for the thief in an honest manner, give him time to think it over, promise him peace by the end of the day, grant him his wish of rubbing his moveable scalp against the rocks in caves that taught him to speak.

2

Stay inside this shell of onions and the holy gourd. It inhabits the trails and the names of those who loved me. It comes from the circle of strong men and women who whispered in sign language and were promised electric violins.

It belongs to the maker of the rosary and the ghost attempting to change his name. It cries in the sound of the glass bird—a one drop eye destined to be awarded a walking cane. There are things to be said besides the evolution of hope and the change in the penance.

Stir the pot with the floating eyelids and the simple boiling soup. It still goes back to food and the way we widen our belts to be able to sing and live. It must be taken back to those who want to wear long, black, wrinkled hands.

Stay inside this shell of newspapers and don't despair. The lone track of the bone thin illness will compensate you for coming this far without revealing every secret stolen by the instigator, the one who cut roads in the desert behind your house, the one who watered the cactus and was desperate enough to tear down his house and cry.

When the first light comes at you, bow down and bleed.
When the first light comes at you, move and paint the mural.

When the first light comes at you, speak in Spanish. When the first light comes at you, give it all back to the thief. When the first light comes at you, make the bed. When the first light comes at you, tattoo your lover.

When the first light comes at you, drink a glass of water. When the first light comes at you, lunge toward necessity. When the first light comes at you, demand a used dimension. When the first light comes at you, let the joy of the black pig inhabit the village.

When the first light comes at you, clean your eyelids of mucus. When the first light comes at you, be impatient and match your extinction with the fresh books of salt left over from the day you learned to correctly spell the family nickname of your father.

3

I recover from the easy things and count the fruit in the trees. I must insist on the long blue tongue of the spider. It has no value other than to feed me when I change the language and become the only son. My sisters having abandoned me to stay with their mother. My father not wanting to see me. My mother wondering why I ran and ran from her. I display the crossing mirror, the style of wisdom and behavior meant for the stolen kiss and the love of peaceful puzzles sounding themselves against my chest as if their vowels were commissioned to employ me.

I recover from the motion of the stalk but don't know how to say it. I recover from the motion of the stalk but don't know how to control the vibration. I recover from the motion of the stalk but don't know how to repeat it. As if it mattered for the bright brown boy to come into the ring and defend his fire against the older men. As if the recovery would give him direction and the ability to swallow. As if the blood punched down the throat would stop the violence. As if the yearning for a hooded crazy shape meant sorrow and thievery. As if the cross meant a crossroad and not a gate. As if the presence of carbohydrates and amino acids meant safety. As if the food of reliance was the food of the stolen wish.

I recover from the named sources that feed me and teach me the blank book. I could be betraying them but I know how long it took them to get here, clean the church, smell each and every corner of the spider. I recover from the tattoo of the blue panther my father carries on his shoulder.

4

When I was told the monkey knew how to make fresh coffee, I had already been converted toward worshipping the vines that brought him down to me.

I was the first one to answer his questions, the only one to place him in my dreams, but I had no idea the thief would hire me as his son, his father, his grandfather who was the best at taking and giving land, adobe, mud, wind, tumbleweeds, and water among those who gathered around him.

When Geronimo died, the white war paint on his face was adapted from the white markings of the flat nosed rattlesnake that lived among his people. When Cochise died, they cut a horse's throat and washed his body in the animal's blood, prepared to hide his burial ground from those who would come after him.

When I died, I was burned in the fire of the cottonwood, designed to be a dust rising from the territories. When I died, the secret markings on the walls were unveiled, translated into a poem that was given time to be misinterpreted, shortened, rewritten to fit into the crushed pollen of the fields where an ash hovered to marry the hummingbird and convince my son there was something hidden in the hard nipples of the father who dies with the sayings that flatten his chest and give him a new body in the manner of the snow.

5

I am only stretching my many feet. One toe was broken when I had no name. The ankles swell when I cross the street. It is not proper to speak about the feet when they have not been washed with honor. It is not the faith in the stepping motion that destroys the clean abrasion embedded to tell the truth. It is being born with both feet twisted in, toward each other like an incomplete animal interrupted from the evolution of hidden demands. And, what about the mother and her deformed hip, which is the well where strange men drink to be able to see, confess, and open their stupid eyes. To behave as if the car of believers is going to stop for me. When you stop don't ask about the hummingbird released by my son who hated to see things hover in the air. I am riding to the field where the rusted cans wait for me. When I show you how to impose your fury and peace it will be too late to turn around and pretend I was never there. Accept the smell. Love your feet.

6

These sayings belong to you against knowledge that a raised window will put a new pair of jeans on you. These callings are designed to convince those who gather that there is a way to be taught.

A manner of lying, of reciting the truth, of exaggerating what is not believed, confusing people until too many new families have been born out of the physical approach to the rosary, the stalk, the whistle, the stolen hoof, the empty cup of holy water,

the empty pew, the stalled car, the missing 45 rpm vinyl record of the first recording of a man and woman learning to breathe, the devised grape and meat left on the table for the first one who enters and takes it without having to recite what was left behind,

the shrimp, the catfish, the squid cut into white shapes containing whole histories of underwater growth the ones who prospered on dry land could have eaten and repeated before every river of their lives dried up,

the vast amount of tortillas eaten to stay fat and pure, lard burning inside the heart, blood vessels churning their scripts against the stomach, the load of shit accumulating and waiting to be dropped over the great tiles of the bathroom in the house of the enemy,

the naked woman insisting this is the only way to put it in, the scarf signaling it is over, the cry of the fingernail still waiting to be acknowledged, the moisture growing between the shoulder blades, the music in the ears full of wax

that changes the tone until the working man comes home and washes and changes his manner of listening, the glass of apple juice, the glass of mescal, the glass of pulque, the glass of milk mixed with the crushed tumbleweed to invade the back part of the brain, hurtle it against the murals painted long ago before the gangs came and sprayed a greater art upon the history of the burned neighborhood.

7

He speaks for the spirit of breath because it is the vanishing point of my hands given and granted by the exclusive yawn toward achieving the shaved head of the heart, the whole motion of involvement and forgiveness—lone wolf, run-down face, interruption beyond need or the salvation of the drifting circle. Passing left and right, asking the entanglement to cease becoming nutrition.

How could I show you what the lake formed in my hands, when all I had was the rapture and the beak of the screaming bird that had nothing to do with documentation? Is this a value grown on my forehead? Will you translate it into the thought where I bury my father, commit myself to the gravestone, and pray about hidden things by making strange, funny sounds?

I can speak about the siren inside the pants of a dead gang member.

I can show you where the bullet entered and became the fountain where all the boys go to drink and be forgiven, so they can grab the gun again.

I can demand an end to the broken street and the mistakes they made in the name of brotherhood, salvation, lust, power, turf, and the manner of coming home at four in the morning to kiss their sleeping mothers on the forehead.

When the flute woman undresses, she takes the theory of sound and speech and places it in the circle that can't be opened without asking. When she sleeps without answering, the cross and the troubled hands give her the meal as danger.

If the baked bread became collected paper, the angry message of stepping from the one-footed owl toward the three-toed monkey would be the missing step of evolution that created twenty or thirty new words for hunger and greed. The vanishing navel of the sister is the vanishing temple of the brother. If some-one gave this interaction a name, they would say everything has been stolen. If someone would believe my script, I could open the other box and begin to unravel what has been melting into canyons and dried rivers for generations. Once, my grandmother fried fresh lizard meat to ward off the starving de-mons of our families past. When we ate the growing meat, we expanded, hurt our stomachs and killed thirty or forty ghosts that were drifting around our house for years.

8

The star between the testicles hits the water. Babies are born already convicted.

When twenty men shake the wind they have polluted their chests with flowers. When twenty women mark the toad they have seeded the head and the heart. When twenty flawed body cells change fate they have molested the electric microscope. When you decide you can't cry, twenty men will weep for you.

Moment by moment, the electric guitar was plugged in and erased the dan-ger of having recalled old songs from the radio. This is the secret ointment. This is the small shoe worn to heal the swollen foot. This is the funny line growing longer between my shoulder blades, two shields named by the Mexi-can tongue, touched by the strange white fingers that have nothing to do with hope.

9

What do they say when the bones are crushed? Do they resemble hope and the fast method of holding onto the brush stroke of discipline? There must be a way to regain the identity of the one who rose out of the canvas to turn the horizon brown.

I struggled with the memory of the bare foot, the nostril in the lake extreme and uprooted, the rich host of milk that dried in my pockets and made me look forward to the white leaves articulating their needles across my back. I followed the cry of the three-legged dog, the happy fellow who ate too much and didn't know women were freed from slavery at the top of his hand, my knuckles swollen from a spider bite, my hair getting longer with the fantasy of angels and the way Jesus Christ negotiated with my maker to leave me alone. I shuddered with the spectacle of the clogged life that came and went into the vision I had of deep clay jars, the ones full of water I could lift in my arms—the ones I couldn't hold and smashed on the ground, their weight more than the water that rained over my head the day I came to count the thirsty survivors. I didn't let you in on the secret of the heat in the mattress, the morning of the virgin becoming the dawn of the first born, a day of dead senses beginning to perceive the world as it made life for the afterbirth, accessible buds of eagerness rising out of the mother to clean the room of coals kept burning for the man who wished his morning of birth had been postponed for years.

10

Here he is with his proud flag of sweat and the pouring vines of home. Here he comes dashing across the grass to see the black butterfly spread its touch upon the blades he cut. Here is the onion, the radish, and the Chinese greens growing beyond the circle of wasps. When he first looked, there was no one to tell him he would be left alone to wish whatever he wanted. When he first decided to enter the ground, no one deposited his seed in many months. It was a way of destroying himself. It was the manner of coming to the bricks and wood and allowing the black widow spider to weave its nest. Across the mutual watering, things spread taller and greener than the difference between fear and breath. These things promise high ground that will never belong to God or those who quit going to church, their greed and circle of believers keeping others out, until they spend their Sundays digging old grass, removing weeds, replanting ground cover that will not expose much as the remains of what he brought back—the secret tumbleweed, the anger of the rose, the nipple of the blackberry bush, the escape of the elephant ears falling to the hot sidewalk to make a leafy carpet of yellow skin that will forget the olives that won't grow here, as the huge leaves dry into a parchment he can't read or understand.

Chicano Tortuga Party

Were you invited to the party?

The Chicano Tortuga party is a mass gathering of people who don't know each other, even though they come from the same families, the strong tribes that have survived mass migration, illegal immigration, and legal (though reluctant) assimilation. The brown people have gathered to look at one another and wonder what the hell they are doing as everybody starts thinking about the end of the century and the next one. The Age of the Hispanic? Who coined that phrase? The media? The party begins tonight, even though it has been going on for a very long time. Ask the homeboys on the street, or the Chicano poets on the soapbox. Ask the Texas politician who just got elected to the state house, marking the first time they let a brown face from that area represent anybody. The party is loud and it is quiet. It is mean and kind. It has to do with food, drink, dress, music, love and hate. It is a celebration of things all Chicanos have and the many things they have lost as they have been slowly taking over the country. The Chicano party extended invitations, yet no one was truly invited. It is a mass gate crashing event, the kind that will make outsiders say, "Yeah, look at those damn Mexicans! Those slick wetbacks. How about those Chuppies with money in their pockets?" The organizers of the party did not give an address. You really won't know where to go. They couldn't rent a hall for the night. Every hall in America is taken, yet there are endless empty rooms in the barrios. Just pull the nailed boards off the windows and climb in.

first tortilla—

We were talking about Carlos and how he wound up in prison for killing Jimmy Rosales two years ago. We kept talking about Carlos and what a great guy he was, how he always showed us the right thing to do when it was a dangerous time. We wanted to remember Carlos each night as we gathered around the parked cars near the old basketball courts. It was a weird time because Lalo and his boys had left the 'hood a few weeks ago. Things were quiet and we didn't know what to do with ourselves. We couldn't believe the fact there were no more dudes in the area. They were all gone—either dead, in prison, or escapees from the 'hood. The four of us were the last ones on Sherman and Nashville streets. I guess we won the war. It took years and at least seventeen guys I can remember are dead or in prison. What the hell, we won the war and this is our home. Who cares if people all think we are crazy and all of us are a bunch of gang members? Who cares if the streets are ours and there is no value in owning the streets? Who cares if the Frito Bandito is out there selling his Fritos, but instead of wearing that stupid bandit outfit with the gun belt, he is wearing a red Bulls T-shirt with a reversed baseball cap on his head? Hey, somebody better teach him the hand signs!

Somebody walks out of the shadows, stops in front of an old car parked on the street, and stares at the boys. He looks like a Chicano in his mid-forties. No one in the 'hood would recognize him. He has been gone for a long time and recently found the courage to make it back. His family doesn't even know he is here, watching their house, thinking of ways to approach these boys and find out if any of them remember Pifas, the tough guy who used to beat the shit out of all their brothers.

second taco—

Freddie and his band got busted last night. They are in jail for selling weed over at North High. This has happened too many times to many of us. It gets real old. I wish I had something better to talk about. La Lorna even told me she saw her long dead grandmother Juana in a vision last night. Things are happening like that around here. People are seeing things they shouldn't see. Julia says it's because none of us prays anymore. We don't even own rosaries. I don't even know how to pray one if I did have one. Somebody told me they saw viejo Chuy down by the Laundromat. That old wino has been dead for six years. What is he doing around here? If old Chuy can come around, anything can happen. I think I'm scared, dios mío!

third bowl of beans—

There is no use in thinking the family will stay together. Ramon is dead. María is in the hospital. Her two sons are in the army and navy. They joined four months ago. Abuela Julia's kitchen is empty. Someone has to break into it and clean it up. There is an old pot of beans on the stove, but they are uncooked. They have been soaking in water for weeks. I can't imagine what the stuff looks like after all this time. The house is boarded up. Even the calendar photos of saints have been taken off the walls. If you look closely, you can see where the paint faded into perfect squares and rectangles where it was covered by the photos. It is almost as if parts of the walls were burned by the power of the santos. San Antonio is supposed to come with his torch. Ramon told me that before he died. He must be crazy like all the others.

we forgot why we even served the tortilla in the first place—

Chew it slowly and taste the oil from your grandmother's hands—the slap happy method of making the flat round dough into plates that will heal. It is made with water and forms a taste that is taste, but as some say, no taste at all. Nourishment that has nothing to do with the expectations that all brown faces eat nothing but tortillas. Stone monuments and artifacts were not created without the Mayans eating the tortillas to build. Campesino. Indio. If you could see how the tortilla cake is your soul flattened in the atmosphere of the new world, you would keep eating them and not eat them at the same time. Roots. Loyalty. Tortillas. Masa. As if you have to bite to see how your people are both hungry and fed. Breast food. Chest food. Heart food. Look at the campesino tucking his tortillas into his shirt as he goes to work. The women folding them in their shawls as they hit the streets. Eat the tortilla. Serve it. Sacrament as if the simple, round, toasted, sometimes burned face of the tortilla is the true reason for gathering everyone together, feeding them what flatness the corn god stepped on long ago. Eating them off the floor of the earth.

fourth calendar photo of La Virgen de Guadalupe—

The howling coyotes came back last night. They circled the adobe house and turned shadows into darker shapes meant to tell our story. I stood by the window and knew Lencha and young Benito were asleep. I listened to the coyotes, but could not make out their shapes in the dark desert night. Something is going on because they keep circling the house. I should ignore their cries and go back to bed. They can sense someone is watching them and it makes them run faster around the small house. I wish everyone would return so we could have faith like we used to, before the other people came and made the world pay attention to what they were doing. The coyotes keep howling.

fifth bead of the rosary—

When Lucha prayed hard, small miracles appeared in her dreams. Sometimes the people she dreamed about came back in real life. This morning she woke and knew Fernando was going to return to live with her by the river. It was a simple thing to think about. Her prayers and her desires would finally be answered. As she yawned and tried to shake the sleep from her head, she wondered why it had taken so long. She did not have any idea where Fernando had been, but she thought she heard his first footsteps approaching her bedroom door.

sixth roll of the taco—

They keep naming their babies after Selena. Since the Tejano singer was murdered in March of 1994, the number of baby girls with the name Selena keeps rising. Mothers and fathers can't get away from it. They want their girls to grow up with the name of the popular singer who has become a legend since her death. Selena. Selena. Of course, this is slightly different than the mothers who are abusing and getting angry at their daughters who have failed to win any Selena look alike contests. Hundreds have been held all over Texas and the Southwest. The young teenage girls show up in skimpy costumes and get to sing and act like Selena on stage. Some of the contests promise singing careers. Others give prizes for the girl who looks just like Selena. Newspapers are running stories on how the mothers of losing contestants take it out on their daughters. The pressure is on to bring back the dead and give the millions of south Texas Mexican Americans something to live for. Most of all, something to dream for.

seventh bite of the taco—

I don't know how it happened, but Tony quit speaking Spanish. One day, he just lost it and couldn't get it back. He grew up in our house listening to Mom and Papa talk Spanish all the time, but Tony's school friends just spoke English. The stupid kid can't even talk to his grandmother Josefina, who doesn't speak English. I can't believe my dumb brother doesn't want to say a single word in Spanish. Hell, even if he wanted to, he can't say the words. He is the first one in our family to be this way. I'm glad I can speak, read, and write it. When I talk to Tony, who is now thirteen, I cuss him out in Spanish. He knows those words and gets mad at me. He calls me a motherfucker, just like all his rapping friends. They listen to rap CDs where every other word is motherfucker. If Tony doesn't start speaking Spanish to me, I'm going to steal his stupid music and make him ask for it back in Spanish.

eight tons of tortillas—

I have dreamed of the river often, but have not wanted to write that much about it. There are too many memories of mud and people crossing, coming and going, wanting to find a place to sleep and eat and survive. I have dreamed of the concrete bridges over the river, their sturdy frames holding the river on its course, the bridges of a spent life waiting for the memories of someone who always watched them to return and believe the river never changes, despite the years of change and the eyes of the polluted strain flowing underwater, invisible touches and frames of anger powering the muddy river to stay as it has stayed for centuries, changing without anyone knowing it has changed course. I have dreamed of the river too often and wonder if the water will always stay dark and muddy inside my head. When I actually go and stand on the banks of the Rio Grande, there is no water. The long ribbons of mud stretch from north to south, the great yearning for constant water as deep as the way I stand there and wait for something of significance to happen—a quick appearance by the first man to ever cross this infinite cut in the earth. When he finally crosses, new families are born along the river—fresh houses of mud going up toward the sun, waiting for several generations to live and die and exist in the vast cotton fields of La Mesilla Valley. When he finally crosses, this man will know why his father told him this was the place his great-great grandfather first gathered a small herd of horses and a few cattle. There is no water. The Rio Grande is a ghost that does not want to hear old stories that have nothing to do with its changing course.

nine bowls of menudo—

Kind speech is a slow flowing spring discovered by Anselmo, a barefoot boy who wandered too far from his family. Kind speech is the first attempt to sound the words that would save him from his family and the secret plans they had for him. Kind speech is the way to describe a wish to recall things that happened in childhood that have been forgotten for decades—daily actions, thoughts, deeds, fears, and thefts that belong in the deep chamber of the brain where the energy spent on committing them would never be repeated again until this moment at the turn of the century when Anselmo's secret respect toward hidden things must be faced, recalled, and relived to find out what went wrong—what power was abandoned and must now be reclaimed before the next millennium ends the dark party.

tenth bead of the rosary (broken but intact)—

There was a time when I thought I could hide in the ground and be mistaken for a tree that would never change color despite the shifting seasons and the breaking years. There was a time when I wanted to be sad and find out what the animal of sadness has to do with my aching knees—the same ones that followed my grandmother as we knelt and walked on our knees, our penance for the miracle of believing there was something waiting for us beyond the heavy wooden doors of the church—the same knees that made it into the sanctuary, the pain of moving a few inches at a time on our knees, the same trembling of power and belief that gave us our names and made us hungry. Even the weeping saints took us in. Even the paint peeling off the face of the old statue of La Virgen de Guadalupe forms flakes the poor gather in their hands to see if the color of faith ever truly fades. There was a time when I had no choice but to follow the old woman as if she kept the part of me she stole from my mother. She kept me as her own since the day I was born. She is ninety-two years old with limited days and I still don't know what she has kept from me. How will I know it before she dies?

eleventh bean plucked from a pile of uncooked beans—

How could I ask myself those questions when I must prepare myself to speak before others and share with them what I know about the roads of words and how they form the map and how they predict each and every closeness we come to before the light that forms wings, angels, hair, teeth, shoes, broken shoelaces, combs, eyes, closed eyes, eyes that don't open, wings, angels, blank paper, bent coins, empty cans, empty street corners where my grandmother used to live before she moved back to my mother's house, corners across the street from the haunted church that I keep in my mind as the image of the barrio that won't leave me because something happened to make my family dwell there, love each other, help one another out, neglect each other, take care of each other year after year. It is as if I have no family because I do not dwell in those rooms. It has been years and I miss that fire, that warmth, that unattainable security I once had because I was not afraid and I thought being part of the family was all it took to survive the church.

twelfth avocado cut by a knife—

I visit my uncle after thirty years. He looks like my father. It is the closest I have been to my father. Resembles. My uncle tells me about the five bullet wounds in his head. Two from World War II. Two from Korea. One from Vietnam. Hero and killer. Nine Purple Hearts. He tells me he killed 82 Japanese in the Pacific. 42 North Koreans and Chinese in Korea. 140 victims in Vietnam. Trained assassin. The Phoenix Program. Two-man teams behind enemy lines. He says the North Vietnamese put a bounty on him and his partner. My uncle who looks like my father. His older brother who took care of him when their mother died when they were six and four years old. He says the day after her funeral they both saw her standing on a street corner pointing to her sons from across the street. They both saw her in the middle of a crowd. My uncle grabbed my father's hand and they crossed the street, but she was gone. They are two men, two ghosts who have hovered over my life without me knowing about it until I was forty-two years old and had to wait thirty years to see my uncle again before finding out which of them is going to acknowledge me first, which one of them is going to get older first, which one will die in silence and which one will know who I am the last time he closes his eyes.

thirteenth helping of habañero sauce—

Tired of describing what it means to come back and be able to register the truth and the opinion of the bad things that left Jose ill for a long time. It has to do with power and his ability to let go without abandoning the artistic world completely. It has to do with wanting to progress toward a self-realized writing that may welcome other people into it, or turn them away without harm. Tired of trying to figure out why the sound of the word has something to do with Jose's memory of walking toward the river and not having any place to go. Too much dependence on the metaphor of rivers, deserts, mountains, solitude, and hot earth. The late Chicano writer Tomas Rivera believed the poor migrant child had to find a way to survive, in order to break beyond the suffering and establish a path toward life, family, and community. There had to be a sense of belonging, of gathering more than one person around the child Jose, and finding a way to escape the harsh realities of migrant life. Rivera used this as a wider metaphor for the plight of many minority children and the racist history of Jose's country. His notion of having to break out in desperation could also be balanced with the notion of breaking free through the time the spirit of the child has taken to age and be aware of a world where the poverty, pain, and racism is an invented way of life that the child has the power to change. Yet, in the long history of Mexican American life, and the history of trying to write about such things, few people have been able to transcend their initial role. Something has been changing with a bolder move toward language that takes the history of people and uses it to strengthen the revised view of what came before, using it also to tell stories of the long-gone to build a path toward something that is here.

◆

Che Guevara

When they cut off his hands to prove it was really him, the soldiers heard the thunder over the Bolivian mountains. It was only a fantasy. It didn't really happen. In the death photo, Che's eyes are open and he is lying peacefully, his shirt off, the hands still intact. Someone across the world says they know where his unmarked grave lies. Someone across the border recalls the last thing Che told him. It must have been the truth, because this person has been in hiding ever since. Once, when I pasted a magazine cover of Che on my office door, a person I worked with tore it down after a few days. He was born in Cuba, told me once how Castro's men ruined his father, destroyed his furniture business, sent his family across the sea. I have many images of Che, often wonder why they inhabit the recent past of many Chicanos I know—this search for his hands. I have several books on Che—once dreamed there was a different leader coming down the mountain. When I woke up, I had nothing to do with this history, but the photo was back on my door, the edges partially torn, a big X drawn across his face, the outline of two hands traced in pen under the beard.

•

Just in time to see the sun hit the red peaks of the Sangre de Cristos, asking if the drum and guitar are still plugged in—

Listening to Carlos Santana on the tape "La Fuente del Ritmo" that Juan recorded from favorite songs of his, all of them over fifteen years old. Older music is the slave to the ear.

"Oye, Come Va!" song: How does it move? When do you move? How is it going when the chata dances naked with you and you grab her and love her and the congas keep the beat!

"Samba Pa Ti" song: Loud, shrieking Carlos guitar escaping into the room of the steaming ears and steaming corn where few go as the high wire act of grimace and ecstatic guitar breaks the belief in the empty places where even the amplifiers sound as if they are going to give birth to an electric kid named Chuy Chamuco Cervantes.

"Flor de Canela" song: Quetzal Bird: Groom of the marriage heart. Invisible creature, legend of electric wisdom worn down by tortilla hands into the Mayan bird of magic and myth and survival. Something red and white flashes in the eye of the man searching for the Quetzal bird in Guatemala. He turns and spots two of the rare birds landing on a nearby cecropia tree. "Brilliant crimson bellies," he recalls. "Snow-white patches under the tails. They were two hens without the male Quetzal's fancy tail plumes. One of the birds suddenly leaped up and grabbed a small fruit from the tree. It hovered in the air for a few seconds, like a giant hummingbird, as it fed. The rapid beating of wings set off a motion of music and color—red and white flashes of light washing the jungle and giving this man a reason to leave."

"Guajira" song: *Vamonos Guajira! Vamos a bailar!* Lets dance, Mama! The party can't be a party without a dance. But, what kind of dances do we perform as the Santana shift tears our shirts and blouses off with searing and accurate intensity. Moving hips and shaking arms, black and brown hair of the crowd shimmering and weaving, losing strands of hair floating in the air as if God was dropping dark confetti on the parade.

"Stone Flower" song: No words. No howl. No refrain. No going back. No reason to cut it short. The long song of moving toward the adobe walls where the true neck of the guitar was first shaped by muddy hands bristling with the feedback moan buried in the mud by hungry Tarahumara Indians long ago. This way north where the hard stone flower grows. Long slide of the gathered adobe on the stage of strobes, Carlos opening his mouth wide to see if the fresh water of the Pacific will cure his endless note of cause and its own cure.

The singer says he doesn't know what to do, then the guitar shrieks like a lost sadness, a fast mourning toward what will never be. Celebrate, but don't ask.

(Three Turtles) 🐢 🐢 🐢

The vato musicians are playing together again. They can't decide if they want to form their own band and call themselves The Incas. Jose is the drummer and brings his bongos and timbales to the garage so Alfredo can join in on percussion. Alfonso is the bass player and is very quiet. He has the most experience in the band and was recently kicked out of Los Tamales for punching the lead singer in the face. Before that, he was with Los Tortugas. Sammy is the lead guitarist of The Incas. His red instrument looks like Carlos Santana's best Gibson guitar. Pedro is the other guitar player and owns a classic Fender Stratocaster.

They quickly jump into a driving, wailing version of Santana's "Soul Sacrifice." Sammy and Pedro cut lead notes and toss them at each other. Alfonso nods his head in steady rhythm, stares straight ahead as his deep bass stays ahead of everyone else. Jose and Alfredo are going wild with the intricate percussion runs, slappings and poundings that made the song a favorite of drummers like them.

Suddenly, at once on the same note, the feedback from the amplifiers and the earthquakes from the two drummers makes the vision of all the musicians turn purple. It is as if they were all wearing purple colored sunglasses. They look at each other above the loud beat and they are all purple. Sammy's goatee is purple. His red guitar is now purple.

There are a dozen kids from the neighborhood hanging around the garage of Sammy's house. When the evening air turned purple and the band screeched, it drew more kids closer to the entrance of the garage. Pedro has some great weed, but nobody has tried it yet, so it can't be the reason everything around them is purple. Their music has made the sky turn purple! The Incas are truly playing together, this latest rehearsal in Sammy's garage the first ultimate coming together of their sound. They are flying as "Soul Sacrifice" goes into a wild improvisational jam, the bass and the drums cracking a canyon full of sound as the guitarists bend their notes and fly into incredible double solos, tearing the purple shirts off their backs with the sheer power of the electric wires that fill the garage floor. The drummer and bongo player keep going faster and faster. Sammy extends a long note that threads above a feedback that would make Santana purple if he was there to hear them.

The kids are still frozen to the doorway of the garage. They have never seen such purples or heard such sounds before. The blasting amplifiers and the shattering drums are driving them crazy. Ten and eleven year olds are jumping and dancing harder on the cement driveway. As their heads weave, purple baseball caps fly off. Even the dancers spot the purple sky above them.

By this time, the sweating musicians are leaning toward the entrance of the garage and straining to look toward the setting sun in the western sky. The band has set up near the back of the tiny room, so they can't really see the entire horizon without having to stop playing. They keep going, astounded their music has turned the whole earth purple. The guitarists are the only ones who can move around the garage with the few feet of electric wires plugged to their instruments. Sammy and Pedro stagger around the floor like they are having heart attacks, their guitars pointed at each other, their bleeding fingers dripping over the glittering guitar picks that vibrate in the purple light. Their long, raw fingers dig deeper into the electrified wires, bodies of the guitars shimmering and cracking with light and sound.

Sammy slams his guitar against his stomach, trips over the trailing wires and screams, "Aye! Aye! Aye! Aye!"

The feedback explodes into smoke. Suddenly, the electricity in the garage blows out with a tremendous pop. There is an incredible electric silence as the leaning musicians stare at each other. Even the drummers stop in mid-blow and just stare. Silence. They don't move because there is no electricity. Silence and a sudden crack in the air. They don't move as they look at the sky through the large open doors of the garage. The sky is still purple. There are no clouds.

They stumble around the garage without saying a word to each other, their legs dangling in the useless wires and cables. They do not know what happened to the electricity. Sammy is speechless and in shock. He has never blown a fuse in the garage before. It has always been the perfect, safe place to practice with the band. They lay down their guitars, the drummers rise, a silent beat slowly fading beyond their burst eardrums. The whole band teeters to the entrance of the garage. The neighborhood kids, stunned at the abrupt death of music, stop in mid-leap and begin to wander off, embarrassed looks on their faces. A couple of them turn with odd expressions on their faces. They can't believe those guys in the garage.

The Incas stand together outside and stare at the sky. Sweat runs down their bandannas, their long hair, their brown faces, and drips onto their soaking T-shirts. They stand in the entrance of Sammy's garage as if they are about to take a bow before a Fillmore audience. The sky is the greatest silent purple they have ever seen. They have no electricity, their instruments are dead, but the sky is a raging, silent purple.

🐢 🐢 🐢

Chuy Chamuco Cervantes —

Chuy came to the party first. He actually set it up. Brought his drum, too. Red bandanna. First son of a father who worked as a used car salesman for thirty years. Lost in El Paso used car lots. Chuy Chamuco Cervantes with the proud voice and the tiny black notebook he carries in his back pocket — his pen has leaked in his pants several times. Inkspots like the clouds that gather over the used car lot of his asphalt dreams.

There are many flags.

Preludio Proyecto Latino: The Cuban jazz pianist Gonzalo Rubalcaba spins a stream of notes toward "Nuestro Balance"—how the Latino crowd is going to be a perfect tool for international understanding, love, justice, jazz in the ear to heal all wounds. Trumpets.

·

A Newspaper Headline in San Antonio, Texas, March 1995:
HISPANIC EXECUTIVES URGED TO GO ON-LINE

The story says that with federal budget cuts, more Hispanic professionals will be fighting to preserve their careers. Felix Garcia, chief of staffing services for the U.S. Office of Personnel Management, held a seminar for over 100 Hispanics in San Antonio. He told them they had to get "on-line" and know how to use the Internet to find job banks and connect to other Hispanic professionals around the country. The emphasis, over and over, was that Hispanics (the chosen word of Garcia's and the San Antonio newspaper) had to quit being "110 percent behind the times" (to quote Garcia). The tone of the story implied Hispanics were still in prehistoric times when it came to computers and knowledge of the high-tech world. Have they ever heard or found the web page on the Internet, created by Guillermo Gomez Peña, titled "Cyber Chicano" and "Cyber Vato"? Don't they know the dudes were wired a long time ago? They have been bristling with megabytes for years! Can we borrow Cyber Vato and take him out of the hall in San Antonio, where Garcia spoke, and invite him to the party?

·

Another Headline:
HISPANICS URGED TO HOLD ONTO POLITICAL GAINS

This is the one we are looking for. The summer before the '96 election and Hispanics are told to hold on tight to whatever they have gained because the Republicans are taking it away and Big Bill may get re-elected without any real attempt at understanding or addressing issues affecting Latinos. Woops! The word Latino. How come the headline doesn't read—Latinos Urged to Hold onto Political Gains? Is the party over, or are we still counting the ballots? Hispanic Gains. The Hispanic Gain. Two or three steps forward and four back. The Hispanic Gain. The Hispanic Pain. The Chicano Tortuga Party.

◆

Not Tortillas This Time, But Latino Yuppie Food

Recipe for a Snack, 1996 Election Night TV Watching:

Banana Nut Quesadilla

4 flour tortillas (there are tortillas!) (8 inches in diameter)
half a cup light cream cheese
2 bananas sliced
2 tablespoons chopped honey-coated nuts
one-fourth cup nonfat caramel sauce or ice cream topping

Lay out tortillas and spread two tablespoons of cream cheese over the entire surface of each tortilla. Top half of each tortilla with banana slices and sprinkle with half a teaspoon of nuts. Fold tortillas in half. Heat a large nonstick frying pan over medium heat until hot. Place two tortillas in pan and cook until golden brown, about two minutes per side. Repeat for remaining tortillas. Cut each tortilla into three wedges and drizzle with one tablespoon caramel sauce. Makes four servings.

◆

Story out of The Daily Tortuga Times:

The Virgin Mary did not show up when she was wanted one night. Lencho told Maria it was going to happen in Austin that day. He said it because he claimed he saw the apparition on the wall of old Julia's house two nights before the whole thing became a public event. When the neighborhood found out, a crowd of 250 gathered by 9 p.m., the time Lencho said the Virgin would appear.

Nothing happened. No Virgin. Nothing on Julia's wall. 250 disappointed and praying people in the streets. Nightfall. Lencho embarrassed, but still trying to convince people he saw the Virgin the night before. Further investigation by several people revealed that the Iglesia La Luz del Mundo, the church down the street, had turned on a spotlight around the time Lencho claimed he saw the vision. People were saying the spotlight hit Julia's house, thus making Lencho think the Virgin was there.

"Even though it was a light on the church," said Lencho, "It is just the faith we have in her. I know that image came from my heart." He told this to several people and even one reporter from an Austin newspaper. To add substance to a story that turned into nothing, the reporter even interviewed Ted Sanchez, a police officer who patrols the East Austin neighborhood. "Even if it is man-made, it's still a nice gesture," he told the reporter. "It did a lot for the community. I'll tell you this, the Friday night crime rate in this area was down dramatically."

◆

Suddenly, 4,812 Cuban "boat people" appear on the horizon, two miles off the Florida coast. Where did they come from? How did they manage to get several hundred small boats and rafts to carry all of them across? Fidel never announced such a thing. Didn't the Coast Guard spot them long before this? They are getting closer. What does this have to do with Chicanos or turtles?

◆

The Body of All

The body of all—a frozen pair of scissors—a withered blackberry bush, the body of all. Staying away from thought, pushing aside drummers who humiliated our response to the song. The body of all—a symbol for electricity— a starving child on the screen—a forest that will not burn—a male tarantula waiting ten years to mate, then die—the body of all. The placement of debt on the floor—Hendrix dreaming of a hummingbird that cries so loud—confusion and ease for the inhabitant who loves to sing, who wants to know. Earn it before it goes. If it is love, the poor go crazy. If it is a coin falling out of the sun, make union with it before it hits the earth. The sense of shutting the eyes before going blind—the body of all. The edge toward peace—the torn Chicano flag—a saxophone dented in two places—an abandoned church crumbling to the ground—the body of Cesar Chavez as the body of all—a ghost standing there every morning—the body of all. The cry of narration—a skip in the fog of grape fields—the focus of splitting the day between sisters and brothers—room to regain faith, the strength to admit they are alone. The party is old. A fear—a mother—a tribe—a brown beret full of dust in the closet—an angel—a pair of ugly twins doing it on the floor—a country coming apart with memory of greed—a tractor following the edge of the huelga—the suitcase— a stolen kiss—the potted plant—a glass of water—the body of all. The next century without secrets and the barrios retreating to rename their streets— Ricardo Sanchez Boulevard—Tony Burciaga Avenue. A scorched house inside this voice—its windows black—its streets wide and full of sparkling pieces of glass—the voice knowing the corners—the story of the neighborhood—the voice not crossing when the light changes—the body belonging there, waiting to be told when to sweat and fit the music of screeching cars—the body not knowing when to cross, when to shave its head, when to sound the call—a bent body staying there—a low body lying there. The next century approaching to level the house—the body of all. The body of all—the body of everything done and undone without knowing it was too late to call.

The Stage: The Brown Star Art Space

The Event: Festival de Libre Pochos

The Players: Grupo Mocoso
(a group of ragtag Chicano actors and performance artists working
the neighborhood)

The Audience: Standing room only 350 people in the tiny,
sweaty theater.

Act One: "Raiz Maiz" with Mara Diaz and Nick Vasquez. Two campesinos working the fields as if they are the last fields on earth. Both of them are dressed in old, dirty clothes and wear straw hats. Is this 1956 or 1996? They are both permanently bent over from years of picking cotton and vegetables in the agricultural valleys of California and Texas.

Act Two: "The Pancho That Got Passed Down" with Tony Juarez, Arturo Fernandez, and Gloria Sanchez-Padilla. A satire of police response times in the barrio. How long does it take a squad car to get to an emergency—a drive-by shooting, etc. The police ask a shooting victim if she is "Mexican-American, Latina, Hispanic, Chicana or other."

◆

Heritage Moment #1

Rosa Martinez, Controller, Los Angeles, California: "The Latino heritage that I have is very strong. My four grandparents were Isleños (from the Canary Islands). I am proud of my Latino heritage, and like a good Latina, I love nature, music, good food and good friends. I am also very spiritual and sensitive. This Latino heritage has helped me excel in a country where you are surrounded by indifference and materialism."

Commentary by Johnny Madrid, rejected member of the Grupo Mocoso performance group. He was kicked out of the party for being too angry. Anyway, here's Johnny commenting on Rosa's statement:

"How can a Latina say she loves nature? What is nature? I can see loving music, food, and your friends, but how many Chicanos, Puerto Riquenos, and Cubanos do you know that have any sense of appreciating nature? When you grow up in the barrio, there are no flowers, trees, or green lawns. Just dirt, mud, adobe, and maybe some potted roses your grandmother is growing on the porch. Love nature? Give me a break. Latinos don't know what nature is. Have you ever heard of a Chicano backpacking tour? How many Chicanos do you know that love to go camping in the woods? Have you ever seen a Puerto Rican going to the ocean to study the tides and think about the extermination of gray whales? Love nature? The only nature I ever got in the Pilsen was when Benny, my brother, who always walked ahead of me, told me to watch out for the dog shit on the sidewalk!"

◆

Domingo's story:

We lived in the fourth house by the river. It was hot most of the year, but Chole and I survived by lying naked on the bed, listening to the mosquitoes, wondering when the river would go down. On the days it rained, we came out of the house to stand naked under the porch. We would laugh, then run out into the mud. After cooling down in the smooth rain, we ran back into the house and tried to sleep. The Rio Grande believed in our house and spared it when it flooded. Most of the time, its dry bed was like a long, brown arm surrounding the house, embracing us like the arm of a giant lying down on the earth to protect us, keep us from wanting to leave and get lost again.

Chole and I had wandered for too long before we found this house. It had been abandoned for years, but I fixed it, repaired the roof and door while Chole cleaned it and got the tiny kitchen in working order again. We lived in the fourth house by the river because it is the kind of place my father said I should live in with the one I loved. He told me how he and my mother had to fight to find their own place to live, why two of my brothers died, how the family finally found peace along this river. It was many years ago. I was still a dumb boy, but remember that most of the people who helped my family are now gone, just like my father and mother, who are dead.

The last time the desert surprised us with its rain, Chole and I had just finished making love. It was around noontime when the sky around the Sangre de Cristos suddenly turned black and the wind pushed against the adobe walls. We ran out to the porch as the sharp raindrops played on the tin roof. Chole and I stood naked, again, laughed because we had been doing more of this lately, and watched the storm hit the valley. Our bodies shimmered in the gray air as we ran around Chole's vegetable garden, the rain washing what we had just finished, the distant thunder making Chole turn her brown neck up to the sky, the steady rain running down her chest like love I could never explain to her. She pulled at her dripping hair, had enough of our cooling joy, and walked silently back into the house.

I paused beside the tomato plants, looked down at myself, and felt alone for the first time. I looked around the fields, but knew there was no one watching me. The other three houses by the river had been empty for a long time. We had no neighbors. Perhaps that is why it was so easy for us to run naked in the rain. Some days, it was the only joy I felt, though I loved Chole and she loved me. As I stood gazing down at my skinny legs, I knew I looked dumb standing naked in a vegetable garden, a man without a job, someone who had to do something fast before we were forced to keep moving, abandon this fourth house on the river that meant so much to us.

When I went inside, Chole had dressed and was sitting by the window. She hardly looked at me and I could tell this might not be a good day to have each other without getting something done. She got mad at me real easily and I always had to watch what I did, so she would be happy and want to be with me.

♦

The smell of oil:

The old woman said she made the world and wanted him to believe each and every sign on the leaves in her bottle of oils. He wanted to believe but didn't know how to let go of the idea that he would not need to learn to read the intricate lines and shadows on the skin of the world she wanted to give to him before she died as the wise old woman of leaves and fallen trees—strong, green cactus greens boiling in the pot on her stove. The smell of the cactus sent him to the moment long ago when he first saw the lines of his body painted on the huge, orange leaf that slowly floated in front of his face as he sat way up in the cottonwood, hiding inside the crude tree house he built the day before. He smelled the lines of his body growing on the leaf as it fell toward the ground, lines and wrinkles of his chest, stomach, and legs winding through the hair on his body, furrows and scars of fallen boys hiding in his clothed body that resembled the leaf abandoning the cottonwood the way the strong odor of her bottle of oils left the air to settle between him and the old woman, until the pain that drove him to the tree house subsided and the orange leaves turned into the dry husks of the winter tree opening above him in search of other smells.

♦

When the faithful wanted to pray, they asked him if they could go down to the river and wait for the black swans to rise and forgive them. He did not know about the black swans, yet he knew they had been with him too long. He granted them permission to go to the river and leave whatever they needed to abandon under the shape of the black wings, the same form he had feared in his dreams for days before they came to speak to him.

♦

Juan of Wands belongs to America. He is the next boy who will gain fame as the new century comes for us. Juan of Wands has friends, but he doesn't know who they are. They sleep while he roams the streets of El Paso, the hot asphalt melting under his Nike feet. Juan of Wands breathes the hot air, then darts under a cement bridge. He left a car tire there. He witnessed a crime there. The homeless man met a switchblade there. Juan didn't do it. He only saw a shadow, but it was enough. Juan believes in the end of the world. He has seen it perish before. It is why he carries a stick in his hand, but it is not a weapon. It is a small, thin piece of wood he found in the street after they took the homeless body away. Juan of Wands carries the stick in his back pocket. It is for protection against those who say too much when he walks in the neighborhood at night. All he has to do is pull it out of his back pocket and show it to the vatos down the street. After they quit laughing and joking about the tiny stick, they get serious when Juan waves it in the air above his head. They stop talking, stare at him because he is the only one among them who has not been shot, stabbed, or beaten. They can't touch him because he is the only one blessed with an old stick from the street. Juan of Wands puts his tiny stick away and keeps walking quietly toward his house. He looks over his shoulder and sees the boys staring at him. He knows something they don't. They know something he doesn't. As Juan enters his house, he is afraid for the first time because he knows, someday, the stick will not be enough.

◆

The ghost of his father believes in coming back with gifts. The ghost is as silent as the living father had been, but insisted on bringing gifts when it appeared one day in the form of a patient man, an old man sitting at the breakfast table, watching the ice form on the windows, waiting for the others to rise from their morning sleep so he could give them the surprise of haunted sorrow, the only kind he ever knew, the source of the sword that cut off his tongue when he was alive. The ghost of his father believes in waiting, in allowing his son to delay the arrival of every single moment they spoke to each other, each second when the truth came out that the world could be inhabited by quiet men who would never harm each other.

•

The small boy watches as the moon becomes a coin in the night sky. The poor angel, caught off guard by the new light, falls from the barriers of wind and clouds, lands somewhere in the Chihuahua desert, transforming himself into a mesquite bush upon impact, anonymous vegetation in the middle of nowhere, one of millions of low, green mesquites the small boy will encounter in his years of walking through the desert in search of the coin he saw plunging toward earth.

•

An illegal in the desert passage (Jornado del Muerto)

Brown wings soar into the twilight above the canyon. They remove the magic trace of smoke and clear desire for seizure. There is enough orange mist left in the sky to see the eagle descend to a high point of red rock, its wings disappearing into the color of the long, stone body. It is the first sign of a rain that does not come to wash the red walls with a welcoming mist. The rain comes to mark the descent of the bird. The eyes that wait for the eagle to land keep their hidden spot on the canyon floor, along a stream that deepens into a running blue that floats through the songs of the moss before it turns green beyond the tight crevices.

The eyes wait on a day when a silent oath to meet the eagle has been made, a promise to go back to the earth and find more secrets to bring to the campfire of the surviving members of the family, carry back those secrets that will heal them from everything they have lost. The family waits for something to happen. They have not been allowed to go watch the landing of the eagle. Only one pair of hidden eyes can wait for something to happen, some movement to change the afternoon, the abduction, the matter of wondering how much hunger has been hiding in the arroyos for generations. There is a change beyond the hurtling light of the red boulders. Even if the old markings on the rocks have never been interpreted, there is the right closure of rock, ocotillo, salt cedar, and limestone to wash the eagle toward the earth.

The bird swerves suddenly above the pine tree line, the patient eyes spotting it immediately. The only echoes in the arroyos are the footsteps clicking on the stone floor, ignoring the shards that wait to be gathered, the missing legs of the dancer fading into the black paint of a call that will never fit the focus of the waiting, hidden eyes. The stream rings like marbles, the song of the moss ending, ripples forming a fresh pattern of descent. The water is unable to reflect the shape of the massive circling wings, now black in welcome for the approaching night.

The eyes blink when a good place for a fire is discovered. There are no broken shards there. No message of revenge will be gathered from the broken pots. There is no reason to avoid the smoke. It is a good place for a campfire. Surprised by the sound of the wings for the last time, there is the realization the eagle has not flown away in the new darkness, but is still searching for a place to land that is not affected by the closeness of the red hands. The red rocks must remain as the red rocks. The fresh cut on the sharp skin of the ocotillo must quit bleeding its green liquid. The black and orange beard of the mountain lion will not be found here. The two eyes are the creators of the lone fire.

Dead tree trunks stack themselves in a cavern of gray and brown, their long branches and collapsed bodies enclosing the narrow walls of the canyon where the eyes blink and wait, a sheer wall of rock rising above the smashed trees that form a box among the fresh mist of a thin waterfall, a line of silver that has begun to dampen the language on the rocks, melting the letters during the long wait, a growing cascade of mist that dissolves the barrier of red earth to come down and drown the empty dryness of waiting. The source of the waterfall is a tiny cloud of flames because the ocotillo and the oldest cottonwood have not stopped bleeding, reflections of the fire that has been built around a ring of stones, flames licking a pattern shaped by the circling wings that are going to descend—the long awaited sign there is a great burning in the air. Eyes watch and ears listen. The rustling of the wings is loud and clear. The eyes gaze up the walls to discover the stars are waiting to see what will be done about the flapping of the hidden wings, a sound so unnaturally close.

The eagle flies low. In sleep or in troubled darkness, the eagle flies low. The eyes know it and wait, huddled before the fire, never dreaming the great bird will come in the night, always expecting a morning stab of pure rock and claw. In the crackling of the simmering sticks, the eyes dance yellow, waiting for the rain of feathers to come down, fall slowly in the canyon air, through the black veins of the powerful tree trunks that witness this lone figure waiting to find the place where the mighty limbs meet and cross each other. Hundreds of years ago, someone gathered shards.

The eagle flies low. It descends toward the figure in the brown serape and yellow straw hat, glides down the narrow walls to perch silently on a thick branch. The eyes open in recognition. The hands open to the descending blanket of feathers, colors unrecognizable in the rearranged night. The flames become small embers and do not flare during the arrival—a crackling, brushing motion with the defiant eyes. One arc. Man and bird are buried in the cool black dust that filters to fall through the branches, covering the smooth red walls, settling before the morning sun can ignite the waterfall in curious light.

◆

Black Jalapeños

The passion of speech becomes the stem at the end of the bite when the black fire is the orange moment in the heart and stomach that hurt with the passion of swallowing the seeds and green skin of the companion. It is a day when I know I have gone past the habit of consumption and I sweat only when my tongue insists it must have a new, black language—a seed and skin caught between my teeth, so I can witness the moment when the first seeds interrupt the earth with their emergence—the black whisper of the jalapeño burning into the solid air of the field, escaping from the mole of the plant to hang on its own, evolve into the thickness of the green fuse. It keeps me from talking too soon. It forces me to bite and sting myself as if this entering is the only way to recall the first green sauce I was forced to eat as a boy—the humming steps of time when the spice of those huevos y tortillas were the only taste I would carry with me. There is no other way to tell it, no other flavor of steam and sharpness to deform the tongue into the jalapeño speech we gather each time we eat. The black jalapeño has its fury and its reason to cure its own lingual touch. It allows me to get past my self-conscious habit of dropping at least two black ones onto every plate I carry to the table. It is a streak of appetite the black jalapeño depends on. I dreamed it when I thought the world had ended its dependence on such a pepper, such a habit of pushing one's own mouth back toward the prehistoric savoring of each and every bite. There is also the dream of the huge canvas bag I found tucked away in the back of the kitchen cabinet, the huge black worms rising out of the mound of black jalapeños. I stared at their hairy movement, contemplated the taste of the worm. Could it be the same as the worm at the bottom of the mescal bottle? Why were these black worms rising from such a hot mountain of secrecy? Did it mean what I cherished most had rotted? Given in to the internal hunger of the caterpillar? Did the faith of chile belong back in the earth? It was only one dream and I have no reason to wait for the next batch of black worms to kiss the black jalapeño and make it whole. Then, I wake to the black bowls on the kitchen table, the empty chambers of tiny misunderstandings, the delightful clay emptiness of the black sauce waiting to fill their hollow air. Even when the black bowls fade in the heat of memory, the tongue still resists and remains, the yellow seeds scattered over the table, the stem bristling with whatever could not be bitten, nor swallowed. There is a sign in the throat that something has been consumed, some calling has been filled with the touch of blackness—the reason for going past the harvested earth to find the soil, roll the bushels of black jalapeños against the hard clusters of dirt, be able to place my lips down near the ground and smell the scorched fever of what will never fade. This bowing can only be hidden between the parted lips, until someone else is willing to kiss the black jalapeño and scatter the black bowls across the black fields of a hot mouth, the stirring water that glistens in the black glasses of quenching thirst.

◆

When the tortuga party ended, there were too many people left in silence. The gathering died down and no one tracked the route of the turtles. Most Chicanos had no idea what he was talking about. They partied and loved and hated and died and passed certain things on to their children and grandchildren. No one knew anything about movements or migrations or the species or extinction. All they saw were the many family members crossing and recrossing the river, whose polluted water killed off the snapping turtles many years ago.

Second Shell

He didn't recall everything about the turtles, but he knew he could not tire of asking about them—even if he had the answers all along. Something came to join him when he first opened his eyes beyond the first country. Something moved among his feet, but he could not look down. The people who partied with him, loved with him, and died with him had left without revealing their own secrets about the turtles. He wondered if too many of them would grow tired of the idea, not knowing it had to be the year of finding out—the end of the hundred years when the first signs would hit the Chihuahua with possibilities. He didn't recall everything about the creatures, but it was the place where he could love, could dream, and go as he pleased, perhaps not knowing that the hidden head of the turtle meant something was still not clear. It lay before him, but the erosion around the cliffs left nothing but millions of fossils he found easy to dig out of the ground, too easy as he stepped into the burden of feeling. This was it, he thought. It had to be the turtle nest he had been searching for. He approached the entrance to the tree, but it was only a tree. He neared the edge of the river, but it was only a river. He came to the current and let the electric sense pass through his body. When he walked away, he was wiser with grief and the realization that he had a place to go.

◆

Witchi-Tai-To

Witchi-tai-to from across the room.
Witchi-tai-to from the dreaming forehead.

Before you arrive, stay late behind the cloud.
Before you believe, keep the city in flames.

They will call you to pick magic out of words
you have never said.

Witchi-tai-to from holding hands.
Witchi-tai-to from cutting your hair.

After you see it, a miniature white room.
After you believe it, a taste of clay on the tongue.

They will know nothing but want you to be there
to show them how to obey.

Witchi-tai-to from a bag of oranges.
Witchi-tai-to from a pomegranate seed.

When you say it, no one leaves.
When you explain it, a guitar surprises you.

They will think you are ascending with passion
and inheritance.

They will repeat it because someone else
is listening to what they say.

Witchi-tai-to in silence.
Witchi-tai-to with care.

When you change its meaning, you deny an angel.
When you change the truth, you whisper it over and over again.

Witchi-tai-to, the dead grandmother has returned.
Witchi-tai-to too many times and you must smear the ash
from burned tortillas across your face.

.

Look at how you reach for things already inhabited—
        formed by the ivory face of gregarious shadow,
how you spin what is written in the sky as consequence—
        molded passage entwined in the murmuring hallway
where you were supposed to understand a common object—
        pelicans unfolding massive white wings, geese disappearing
above clouded fields, the lone deer entering your yard in trouble,
        one lone coyote running the opposite direction of image—
how you must have seen these things and waited and thought.

Look at part of the flower without asking what happened—
        calcium appearing to ward off the worm and the seed,
how the day weighs its dawn of indifference and calls you—
        there must be a few ways to move toward the corner:
blending the whistle with the carved tooth of a dog, the empty wine glass,
        a sunken portrait of the charging horses with Sioux warriors
screaming for the soldiers to stop running so they can kill them—
        the place where you must have dreamed of revenge,
skies following the river past the outstretched men of sleep.
        There is a purpose here—a flute being dismantled,
lips of the blower calling you to listen to her questions again and again:
        What shall we do with the day?
Who will cross into the idling car first and go to sleep?
        How can you love the image of quiet priests
when they tortured you with candy and the steaming crucifix?

Look at what you have left to tell the hushed crowd—
>how it sinks and waits for the end of disbelief—
There must be a way to say this and keep the flower.
>There has to be time to measure the spiderweb and kiss.
Someone will have left you a message by now:
>Its first few words emerge from the startled blood of jars:
Hurry. Hurry. Be lost and caught and safe and careful.

>When this message is pronounced, you answer.
When you look at what remains, you will have been serene,
>only a replica of measure kneeling down on the black floor
and folding your hands together.

◆

A meandering, vagrant line.
>In which the mind takes its time.
A night air for all our lives.
>In which freedom returns as a dark act.
A close saxophone trembling with doubt.
>In which love is tunneled into the heart.

>*It costs two centuries.*
It takes an eternity to reassemble what was stolen
>when you asked the earth to travel
and rattle your faith with the end of the century.
>*It costs twenty hours.*
It has to do with the rain and the flooded street
>and it escapes you without reason.

From behind the moon, the human skull shows its passion.
>From between the legs, a starfish.
From in front of the dance, the human cripple is intimate and loud.
>From what he has learned, a birth.

From above the city, the human tower of sex and the unified tongue.
> From inside the thumb, the charity to take it.
From below the womb craving for air and the only shoe, a language
> burning on a hinge of delicious space.

A straight, well-thought line.
> In which the mind convinces the hawk to follow.
A weary ritual to hail the mother.
> In which the open mouth inspires.
A circle of prayer to house the blind.
> In which strength arrives from all directions.

Holy Garcia

Holy Garcia stood on the edge of the desert and prayed that he was okay. He had walked across the Jornado del Muerto without any water, staggering over one hundred miles of emptiness—the canyons, sagebrush, and cactus meaning nothing to him. Holy Garcia removed his helmet and stared at the long ribbon of blue water as the unnamed river fled past him. He had no idea where he was and had not seen the others in days. He stumbled forward and leaped into the river. It was a shallow point and he splashed into it without thinking. His knees sank into the soft mud and he felt himself being swallowed by the silt as he drank and drank. He fought to pull himself up, stumbled back, and managed to crawl onto the bank. He lay there gasping for air, half his body covered in shiny black mud. He closed his eyes, wanting to sleep, but heard a loud noise beyond the cottonwoods that lined the river. He sat up slowly and his vision cleared in time to see the long parade of naked people as they came out of the tall reeds. Their bodies were painted in many colors and the men wore bright feathers and what looked like the dried skins of lizards and snakes on their heads. The women and children stopped and stared at Holy Garcia, while the men, some of them holding spears and clubs, surrounded him in a semi-circle—the river to his back. Before he could wipe his long wet hair from his eyes, two of the naked men grabbed him without hesitation and threw him into the river. Holy Garcia saw the blue sky for an instant as his body arced back through the air. He fell into the shallow water and his back hit the bottom. He tried to cry out in pain, but swallowed water instead. He came up for air, his arms thrashing about, his stinging eyes barely making out the row of brown people who stood on the bank and watched. The two men who threw him in entered the river and held him down with their spears as a third one—this man wearing five rattlesnake heads on his chest—came forward. He pointed to Holy Garcia, who suddenly felt a tranquil, peaceful surge of force go through his starving, frightened heart. The two men in the water nodded to the third as they both buried their spears into Holy Garcia's chest. The third man, his arms folded over his chest, became a sixth moving rattler as Holy Garcia fell back into the warm currents. He handed his mother the rosary with the red beads, pressed from rose petals, and silently bowed among the rows of young boys receiving their first holy communion in the crowded and silent church.

•

Always when I think of the cottonwood
and the black drawings on the rocks,
two worlds inhabit the yellow grasses.
In one, I am afraid and running
across a shallow, dry river.
In the second orbit, I hang onto charcoal
and mark my own walls with hope.
I feel the years of rock and cry
because I don't understand alphabets,
how the triangle and arrow penetrate sandstone
to enter my eyes and rewrite history.
I feel the lines of the *ocotillo*, cut my hands
so they bleed symbols that make sense
only to those who speak aloud,
voices tasting the cave for the first time.

Always when I see the thought
becoming a huge willow,
I answer and stop and need.
When I ask the branches for time,
there is one cricket and a handful of chalk
from the walls that fell in.
When I leave without shade or leaf,
I hear the sound of water,
the arrival of speech, nothing else I need.

.

Once the barefoot man

came to the edge of the village, crying since birth and war,
calling to his mother to identify his swollen hands, his swollen brain —
gray hair from years of asking the peeling statue
of La Virgen to join him for supper.

In the mud and in the glass of broken bottles where he walked,
his feet knew the ground and gave him a chance to smoke.
When the barefoot man fell down, no one looked and no one helped,
because his basket was empty and knew no bread.

Once the barefoot man got up, and it rained in the village
for three days, the flood washing his feet, stranding him
on the edge of a roof where he looked down, howled
like the last dog they shot when too many dark paws moved in the streets.

In the black lake of water, from the roof of a stranger, the barefoot man
learned how to step without help or La Virgen or the need to weep.
When he swam to the end of town, his eyes were like red moons
and he had no reason to use his feet.

•

Let us remember where we came from,
so that we can hear pieces of paper being folded,

so that we can identify our hunger and the whiskers
on the chins of our fathers as things that disappeared,

so we can find the worried mother in her blue dress
ironing a thirty year old wedding gown again and again.

Let us save tomorrow for health and hot food.
Look at the spring and how the snow screams.

It is still falling because we can't imagine heaven
and heaven doesn't wait for us to give up everything we feared.

Tomorrow we won't want this any longer.
We will be strong with long hair and fresh tomatoes

sliced to look like circles of stars we consume,
their taste the taste of anger when rage was a gift—

a dazzling silence that writes the question and
burns like a child excited that everyone has returned.

•

Diego Returns

Diego returns and paints turtles on his cheeks, one tiny green one on each fat
jowl. He recalls how he used to buy tiny baby turtles in the pet shop and bring
them home, setting up a small, stinking aquarium with dirt from the garden,

setting water in a dish for the tiny things that only lasted a few days before dying and drying up before Diego's eyes. He kept buying the baby turtles in the pet shop, some of them only two inches long, but could not keep them alive. He finally gave up and started painting turtles all over his room, the walls, the covers of his schoolbooks, on his arms, even an intricate one on the inside of his thigh, until too many baths washed it off. Diego returns and looks in the mirror as he washes his face. He looks up and sees that he does not look like himself any longer.

◆

I was surprised.
I didn't know communion was danger.
I had no idea the frost of the eyebrow commences to love
and borrow the tune from the dying blade of thorn.

I was involved.
I had to escape the parliament of sweating heads
and trace love inside the cup of not knowing what to do.

I was afraid.
I saw a figure move through the borrowed gate.
It came toward me without surprise or faith.
I feared it would take me and give me the gift of sound—
        how the entrance to the stream surprises,
        how the step into the mud molds the heart,
        how the music of the teeth feeds the loss.

I was brave.
I moved out of the way and the shadow passed.
It became the vessel on the snowy mountain.
It was the crazy mantle of choices, the proud rocks
tumbling toward the edge of the cliff so horizons could forgive:

Forgive me for talking about what I don't know.

Forgive me for asking to be considered.

Forgive me for the swaying spirit that sees its own nature.

I was talking.

I stepped forth and gave the sparrow a dim field in which to peck at the ground.

I allowed two languages to recite about the heaven of whales.

I did not refuse the story of the man who healed himself with years of not talking.

It was a photo of a woman I loved standing on a pile of rocks, pointing to the stars.

It was the repetition of the rain and the wait for memory as if nothing goes wrong.

I was surprised.

I had no idea I had to wait for the grandfather horse to overhear the blue bell.

I did not know the river made a sound like someone's fault.

I was there when the city of speech gave thanks for a whisper and a call.

I was the one who called and the one who never answered.

◆

Graffiti Claws

They found the painted walls and doors and cars and streets and did not know what to do about it. They saw the dayglow green and orange and white and thought about the tears that had flowed for many years — the bewildering form of letters fat and tight against each other on the sides of railroad cars. They walked their neighborhood and found the strange words illuminated every front door on the street. People came out and stared at the incredible style and comprehensive invasion of their homes. The graffiti was everywhere and no one had noticed when it happened. The entire row of houses was covered in some manner. They stood in the street and in front of their houses and stared.

Most of the words and slogans could not be understood by the people who got angrier as they realized how they had been violated. The police were called, but no one knew who had tagged the area. This had never happened before, though several people had seen occasional graffiti down at the corner where Lucha's grocery store used to be. Families spent several days getting rid of the graffiti, some of the damage irreparable without new doors and fences, though most people chose to paint over the dynamic letters. Three days after the last house was clean of damage, at approximately one o'clock in the morning, a brief thunderstorm passed over the town and dropped a strong rain. As the dark clouds moved beyond the neighborhood, the few people who were awoken by the storm did not bother to look outside. If they had, they would have seen the miracle of how the rain and wet surfaces of buildings and cars and fences were slowly bringing back the graffiti they spent thousands of dollars covering up. As soon as the first person unable to go back to sleep would look out his or her window, he or she would be surprised and dismayed at how easily the pure and natural cycle of the rain brought the alphabet back into their lives, the dayglow combinations of green, orange, and white giving extra light to a neighborhood that always gave in to the darkness of unpredictable, brief weather.

◆

The imagined starlight is there,
readjusting its necklace of galaxies to fit the anger
deposited by the god who loved me,
signed my forehead with laughter and language—
the real streak of wealth is there,
zooming into the anguished mixture of herbs and delicacies—
zero taste for the endless mother who capsized lives,
gave her sons twisted roots and cornfed animals
to worship tongues and stomachs upon.

Distances, maps, hands full of soil, how they must be opened
and inspected by the bearded apostle who loves me,

the one who wrote trees and mountains, composed countries
so wars could take their time destroying men.
The imagined starlight is there,
beaming its story into a cup of ruined mahogany,
black vein I have carried with me since a child,
the tree from which the railroad was built—
first engine calling the expecting rain to turn into storms
of parrots formed when lies were no longer enough—
they only kept a few boys going, a few young things
from hatching stories out of their secret joys.

The real comet is there,
fastening its wind to the chair of wounded tribes—
histories, conditions, cold fires, tired messages decomposing
upon the backs of poorly built houses, white balls
of fur flying off the cottonwood to startle the eyes
into thinking it is snowing, it is falling and yes,
there are places to go where heaven has been.

♦

The boy who told stories burned his toast every morning. His mother insisted on making it for him, but he refused. He had to be the one to put the two slices of bread in, set the dial on dark, and waited for the burned toast to smoke and pop up. It crunched in his teeth every morning. The voice told him that black toast was the secret to telling good stories. Once, he told his friend Nemo about the skeleton in the swimming hole. Nemo didn't believe him, so the boy took him there to prove it was true. The place, a swamp off the river, did not have the usual group of naked boys jumping in. The boy who told stories pointed to the skeleton at the deep end of the hole. Nemo had to strain at the edge of the water to see down into the green, murky cloud. He didn't see a skeleton, the other boy claiming it was the missing kid from Bowie High. Nemo looked again, but saw nothing. They finally left and the boy who told stories admitted later he had made the whole thing up. Nemo punched him hard on the shoulder. When the boy got home with a big bruise on his left arm, his mother noticed and scolded him. "Telling stories again?" she asked him. The boy nodded in tears. She made him sit at the table and told him she was going to make him some toast. She did not let him set the dial. Two nice, light brown pieces of toast came up. The boy's mother set them on a plate and pushed the butter tin and knife toward him. The boy who told stories told his mother there was a long, black hair on one of the pieces of bread. She didn't believe him because he constantly made things up. This time, it was true, but she didn't see it. She told her son he had to eat the snack or he couldn't go play with his friends for one week. The boy went ahead and ate the toast with a strand of his mother's hair stuck on a nice, thick line of butter. After that day, he never ate burned toast again.

•

The moans of the river woman

She arrives with a pine cone between her breasts,
looks at me and shakes her head.
She has the time it takes to open the wheel
and insert a bellybutton full of pollen
into the heart of the confused man.

The moans of the river woman rise with power,
song, and greed.
She takes her time inventing butter and sausages
from the carved bones of rare fish.
She takes her time because I am there,
waiting for her to love me, never leave me,
give me the few words needed to say this:

When I loved, I waited across the street,
wet legs and arms glistening with desire.
When I loved, I saw the vegetable hanging on my lips,

its green threads composed from God's throat.
End of a few words.

The sounds of the river woman interrupt me.
There is a parade of sparrows and crows circling
around the bridge where she crossed.
When she disrobes, there is a mountain.
When she makes another sound, I am going to
leave her with an idea influenced by necks and shoulders:

This is it and this is how I survived.
I tried to build a pyramid of bone,
dancing around it in secret so nothing would explode.
It was only my secret desire, my hot load
opening the water to the river woman
who has no name, no face, only the mark of the lover
who knew me and threw me across the current
without letting go.

◆

She moaned and called the turtles. No one believed it because they were tired of the legend. They didn't want to hear her crying anymore, wishing for strange things that could never be, learning the cold worship of kindness from her son, not her husband, but her son. She moaned and called the turtles, but no one bothered to see if any came out of the air, the ground, or the sky. No one looked when she gathered huge, heavy things in her arms and staggered away.

◆

Against the running white meadow of hands,
watch the strike of lightning bring them back
across the country of familiarity,

without pause, see the storm carve
the sentence mistaken for testimony.
It gives those hands a chance to touch.

How slowly it builds upon its sadness.
Three murmurs and a speeding bullet
sick of its place in the brain.
How often can you love this plot,
this bath, this lack of heaven
in the ashes painted on your face.

Between the thought and sacrament,
under the heaving palms of ice,
there is a small fortune crying for
a wah-wah pedal to smash the heart
with a reason to stand up alive.

Man tearing at his spirit

He pauses at the end of the century,
arrives slowly where he has been.
The need to empty the mind,
cherish the heart with white roses,
the erupting flight of too many crows.

He tears and tears, sees himself
in the mirror of canyons,
running toward the last town
where beauty waited for him—
forms of women and envy,
proud stallions falling
into the dust because dust

was only temporary,
running animals carrying
his spirit out of him.

He starts to empty what is left,
sees there is more to gain
by slowing down beside the scent
of what came before:
mountains turning brown,
spiders building knots
of hair in the chests of men,
objects terrified by untongued
voices calling for him to stop
what he is doing, look at his hands
and wait for the likelihood of touch —
the way the crescent birthmark
on his chest closes the hissing spirit,
keeps its woven secret from totally
escaping his nourished frame.

♦

A man could say, "The Maya haunted me.
I didn't understand how those stone masks
were my grandfather full of hate."

A man could stare at the museum of his hands,
find his mother sacrificed
on the stone slab of his forehead.

He could say, "The Maya left my right nipple
and settled in the valley far
from the desert that owned me."

He could climb the vines and find no one,
think he is in the wrong country when
horses surround him with colorful flags.

A man could say, "The Maya are the ones
frozen in the books.
They have nothing to do with me."

He could admit his mother's family was slaughtered
at the border, their bare feet sticking out of the ground
the day the museum of the forehead burned down.

◆

Aguacate Eyes

He saw her standing in the doorway and he recalled the green light in his heart, how his own eyes had been stranded by her memory. She stood there and stared at him, her long, brown hair combed neatly as always. He thought he smelled the sweet scent of aguacate, but all he could really find was her presence. He rose from the bed, but she motioned with one hand for him to stay. He hesitated and watched her slowly turn her back on him and leave. It was not what he wanted, but the aguacate slices in the bowl let off a tender magnetism as they sat waiting on the table near his bed. He rose and heard the door close gently. He picked up one large piece of aguacate and put it in his mouth. The taste he loved made him think of the time they sat in the Mexican restaurant waiting for one of them to make the first move, say the first thing that would drive them crazy and make them want each other. They had both ordered guacamole salads before the main meal. He had always hated guacamole because he loved fresh aguacate in its original form. Now, as he ate several slices from the bowl, he realized why she had left him. It was no longer a secret and something that would eat at him. He set the bowl on the table and sat back down on the bed. He waited for the phone on the nightstand to ring, but he knew it was too soon for her to try to call, perhaps say something that would save them. He caught the smell of the aguacate again and turned to the tiny, white bowl on the table. It was empty, but he knew he had left three or four large slices in it. He rose again and approached the table. The plastic bowl was empty. He picked it up and held it to his nose. The smell of aguacate made him close his eyes and see her hands grabbing the tortilla chips as she dug into the guacamole salad. After she took the first bite, he saw a bright smear of green on her lips. He set the bowl down on the table and waited, with his eyes closed, for her to wipe her mouth with her napkin. When she did, he opened his eyes to a new smell of green, cut aguacate that filled the room with things he wanted to taste.

◆

Burned Tortilla Text

Belinda cooked the tortillas and saw several faces on them that day. She thought her family would think she was crazy if she told them at least three faces appeared on the burned part of the tortillas she made in the kitchen of their tiny house. She had heard stories about Jesus appearing on some tortillas, but never believed it until now. The first face she saw on one large, thick tortilla was the face of her father. He stared at her as he had done when he was alive, rarely talking to her when he would come home tired from working as a used car salesman. He died eight years ago. The second face was the clear, heavy face of Belinda's first husband—Lalo. He was killed in the Vietnam war and she saw his face in many places, but Lalo had never come to her in a tortilla before. His dark, brown eyes were as cutting and curious as when the two of them had dated in high school. He seemed to stare at her harder than her father, so she quickly slapped that tortilla on top of the stack, hoping one of her children would run into the kitchen, grab it, and eat it. The last face Belinda saw that day was her own. She was a proud woman in her late forties, the wrinkles and deep, green eyes appearing near a rough edge of a tortilla. She looked at herself and wondered how many thousands of tortillas she had baked in her lifetime, yet only these three today brought faces to her. She looked through the two dozen tortillas she had stacked on the plate. Sure enough, the three faces, including her own, were clearly branded in black burn marks on the light brown flour. She took the three tortillas, wrapped them together in wax paper, then went to the front screen door. She looked out and spotted Don Fernando working in his garden across the street. Before her children could come and interrupt, asking for dinner, she went out, crossed the street and merrily gave Don Fernando the fresh tortillas. He was a widower and she often brought him plates of her delicious food. He thanked her and told her he would have the tortillas that night with dinner. She went back to her house and started the meals for her children. When Bernie and Linda came and sat at the table, she served them, then went to the door as they ate. She looked across the street and found what she knew she would see—Don Fernando fed the three tortillas to the huge parakeet he kept in a cage on his porch. Belinda watched as the old man tore her three tortillas in small pieces and fed the bright green and red bird, who delighted in the meal as his squawks echoed across the street, the smell of fresh beans and more tortillas pulling Belinda away from the sight.

•

Rhythm Flag

red truck passing down the street
gypsy guitarists on CD gunsights
howling about Spanish love
forgetfulness
yellow leaves falling as if this is it
roofman next door with metal ladder
trying to climb onto the roof
no one home
no one sees him disappear
blue van passing down the street
stack of new books tottering

this is going to hurt like hell
he says it is going to hurt because voices repeat themselves
he says it has to do with love and yearning
this is going to become a lark

◆

the face I saw when I was left alone
the heart I pulled at in my sleep

some woman telling me about sacrifice
smiling as if I was the one to take her
teach her how to get to the top of the pyramid
remove the star from her nipple and worship her sorrow

when I got up without breath
one streetlight burned two thousand years before its invention

◆

old Chicano poet drinking
appearing in our midst
crying old songs
wondering why the young crowd
knows nothing about the streets
the old cries
old banners proclaiming new brown skin
old black poet mesmerized by love
sweating under the banners
asking his god to forgive him
for too many thoughts
against his own people
old black hands

the old cries
coming back to destroy the haunted heart

•

rhythm flag
rhythm posture
(there could be sorrow here)

rhythm fret
rhythm guitar
rhythm master
(he learned to play the flute)

rhythm heart
rhythm forgiveness
rhythm state
rhythm goodness
(rhythm evil was denied)

rhythm education
rhythm mistake
rhythm margin
(he will find the direction and uncover the evolution of what loves him)

rhythm fold
rhythm amusement
(he asked for wisdom)

rhythm flag
rhythm knees
rhythm father
(the only mother must have been the first)

rhythm money
rhythm talk
rhythm opinion
(demand a heavy price for)

rhythm body
as if I could repeat it and have everyone believe me
without having a need to hear the same sound over again

the same words we lost when we refused to vote
vindicated when the rhythm vote destroyed the world

◆

Once when Juan said the guitars were moaning in the pawn shops, no one be-
lieved him, their backs were hurting, they had kissed the migrant fields too
long, their backs bent over for decades as if the moaning guitars could be found
among the rows of grapes rotting in the sun. When Juan said the spoken wheels
of our fists belong to our history, his people finally understood and sang to the
sound of the broken beat, a sweating howl at the vanishing fields of black tor-
tillas burning slowly to reassure us the roads we walked were already marked

◆

She left me a shield orange and light brown rough circle with tiny figures of
Indians hunting elk three wolves crossing the tundra in the middle a framed
scene of the giant hunter throwing a spear into the snowy air two more wolves
running at his feet the three of them running together over the high snow
clouds distant gray trees bending like her arms bent toward me and pushed
me over the cliff so I could come home and be the wooden carving on the shelf
high above the head of the sitting man the spitting man the handcarver who
is always there to shave the truth out of the boy

•

Old woman pushing a grocery cart across the street going to the store dressed completely in black shoes black stockings and skirt black shawl black scarf draped over her bright sun on a bright day suddenly the black figure of the old woman pushing an empty grocery cart across the street her head turning in all directions as if she is afraid someone is following her old woman in black the day turning brighter with the black figure

•

the electric eye of transformation
the swallowed vowel amusing the throat

two fingers dancing in the dark
three flying geese landing on their heads

the electric eye of transformation
behaving as if forgiveness is a color of the earth

as if the sleeping canyons wake with pause
rain on themselves to settle their trembling future

spreading hands on the landscape masking desire
by showing me the way to the carpeted dawn

because I am the last to know the last
to amuse myself by walking on the edge

until I say the cold pockets of my father
are the same eyes that started the harvest

until I say the cold anger of the shadows
is the same color as my receding hairline

until I say the cold fashion of the wires
is the same puzzle carved on the adobe walls

until I say the warm surprise of inventions
is the closeness associated with love and loss

until I say the casket of broken corn holds
every single tooth pulled out of tired, old men

until I say the summer of music and caution
is the season when I finally got up and ran

◆

Five Askings

It was a place where lizards stepped on waxen ground and trees grew tortillas
as if they were the only food that could open the mouths of thieves—a house
where the arms of sleeping babies glowed blue with the milk of angry mothers
who swept too many floors—the moment the thorn invented a penetration
that was kept secret, a spot on the skin where heat dissolved desire, kept side-
walks open for the sun to part. It was simply a room where the open windows
massaged the walls with lies, smells that rose from a bed where something
moved, the sky slapping shut the black clouds that believed possession was
creation—every place like this the room where I was born.

Imagine the glow on the bed sustaining itself, collecting remorse, opinion for
the language of forgotten deeds where you belong and can't be taken away.
Going there becomes insistence, the very thing that happens to you. Imagine
how the fist in the water causes landscape to twist, miles of forest burning be-
fore anyone can find the rest of the world. How often do you think of this?
How soon will the man and woman imagine the house and make love inside?
When one door is parted, they step inside and dwell there for many years.

Wide open fury of ages and graying hair. Inside the church, a music eats itself. There is no time to recall the first language of sin. It has to do with crossing the sanctuary as a child and reaching the altar as a man. Men with open arms are crucified. They have nothing to do with sin or desire. They teach lessons and obey the clouds, know how far to ascend to impress the fearful, the weak, the repeated oaths. Deep shadow despite confession. Inside the oven of the brain, an admitted error. Crossing toward the candles, there is no one to stop me. I have swallowed wax and consumed ashes, the manner of uncovering my head, smelling incense that changes the walls, the holders of voices and prayers denouncing the existence of bread.

Waiting for the dead cactus in the pot to come back, I learn to wait. I stay up nights, think of my first Beatles 45, a song I sang when no one was around, a tiny vinyl record that disappeared years ago. Hoping to remember the words, I touch the thorns in the rotting plant. The sharp reminder puts me to sleep, guitars ringing in a studio somewhere, my chance to sing before a crowd disrupted by this quick dream where people pay to see me, boo me off the stage, wake me among a stack of 45s lying across the floor like crushed wheels of a car that blared its radio as I swerved to avoid the lights of fortune and fame.

There was a tree where I used to go stand as a boy. It was hit by lightning, but I never heard it. I woke weeks later with a beard, long hair, a weight in my heart I carry to this day. What I overheard had everything to say about the vanishing point where I no longer needed to see. To this day, I don't see—only take what is given, rearrange the vowels to fit what really happened when the size of my head changed and I woke up healthy as a crow.

◆

Someone is missing from the tribe
They are searching for him
He used to be loved
He wore colorful feathers in his hair
His face was two or three faces

Sometimes he appeared as four men
Always slept as one

Someone is missing from the fire
They are deciphering the smoke
He was not loyal
He had too many gifts

He wore the language of his family
between his nipples
He coughed and made up new words
He was told not to stay if he ran out of breath

Someone is missing from the tribe
They are searching for him
He used to stand right here

His feet left something in the mud
His feet twitched and the dawn came

His guitar

He was strong and finished. He was available. He gave speeches and saw the clouds come back. He answered questions and wrote prayers to the wind, strummed a guitar he found in the alley one day. It had a strange carving on the wood and looked like two hands with finely drawn fingers beckoning someone to play. It was like the silence that was tightly wound on the strings had nowhere to go, but away from the tossed guitar. He was strong and played, but he didn't know what he was playing. No one heard him play the song he knew. His fingers had callused long ago when he used to pick the tune every day. Now, as the carvings on the body of the guitar creaked and changed their pattern, he ended his song. The guitar was no longer a stray instrument. It could not be called an abandoned thing. When he finished, he listened to the

last sound of the strings and watched the fingers on the guitar come out of the
wood and take their own shape.

                                    ◆

Don't tell me what you are doing
        don't kiss my city
and tell me to go away
            don't lift the skirts of the river
and pretend it is a woman
        wanting water to pass from your lives
until it diminishes you into valuable secrets
           the two of you can take to your bed
assume the position of love is foaming
        at the edges of a terrible mountain

Don't tell me how the cold darkens the moon
        don't blend your kiss with the fate of sparrows
they remove themselves from the picture
           without losing too many of their flock to the current
wanting us to ignore the fact we are in the city
Don't tell me the sound of laughter burned you
        don't pretend the answer led to the end of the century
and changed the history of one person
           don't open your hands without the bottle of glowing water
you scooped from the slow river
        don't drink it before the first cloud sits over our heads
reminds us we are already electric and drowning

                                    ◆

as if the monster in the photo was alien and no one had to believe it was drawn
by a little boy afraid what he was dreaming came true

and the fantastic joy of having a creature to control destroyed the will to be
a perfect son who would always pray and be loyal and know when to leap off
the toilet

•

Where are the men who could have taught me the mirror is always in front
of my face?

•

My voice came from Paradise,
went into the canyons and changed.

When I thought I saw Paradise,
I was wrong.

It was only the sand blowing inside my head, transforming me
into the sensitive man who gave up his red face for a stranger one of brown.

My voice came from Oblivion,
went into a dive beyond the easy waters of my mother—

casting forth as symbols painted on wrinkled legs
and the irons by which the slave labor built the town.

My voice came from Confusion,
when any man receives himself as the true sadness trembling in the fist.

•

The unguarded lion stands there and watches me.
I fed it too much ice cream
and it has returned for my heart,

only my heart that whispers the truth
and convinces the unguarded lion
I am worth the excursion.

It does not move, stares at me
as if the final leap will be
the first ring around Saturn.
I take a couple of steps back.
Its tail twitches for an instant,
the only movement from this huge thing
only twenty yards from me.

The unguarded lion has recited
my poetry before, but is not that good
at remembering every word,
or passing it on to the next generation.
I can't tell if it is hungry,
but I am going to love this lion.

I have no choice—its huge paws
are larger than my head
and would be perfect ornaments
at the foot of my bed.

•

He says his knees are fueled by wonderful fireflies and he illuminates the
jungle as he goes trampling through the villages of love and melting families.
He says his hair is the nest of mad sparrows. They shit in his eyes every day
to grant him sharper vision, let him see the world for what it is. He says he
loves everyone, but sleeps with only two, an old woman of golden armor and
a young girl of magnetic life, whose breasts remind him of his mother's. Her
cries in the night frighten the frogs into a terrible, new army. He says he is
searching for the right country, a home without a flag or banner, a people who

take off their clothes to cover themselves with leaves, a family who will surprise him in the morning and tire him at night. He says his ugly head is too big, but it fits in the river when it is time to join the turtles and go floating slowly toward the sea when the light in his knees gives out and the hummingbird in his brain dives into the flower.

◆

Hidden in the museum, the bowls of the first people sit on metal shelves, crack in the dust of discovery and excavation, row upon row of white, black, and brown pots lined up without room to be displayed. The guide says the twelve thousand clay bowls must stay in storage until they find more space, the collection taking one hundred years of digging to gather, pots surviving the doom of the people to be uncovered and tagged on a shelf. One large bowl carries the worn head of a bird, perhaps an eagle. It was sculpted out of the need to call its might and protect the grain and the seed. Its head stares off the rim, the beak guarding against erosion, against the fish of dirt that wraps itself around the rows. The number of pots holds the eagle as if its cage of clay will break, the shuffling of pots done without tools, the exact cracking of shards sending the eagle on its way.

I found the fossils after a desert rain, walking in the arroyo with my head down, my feet in the soft mud. It was easy to bend against the slipping walls and pull flat rocks into my hands. I rubbed the mud off to find hundreds of miniature shells petrified in their sea. I never knew their geologic names, but saw creatures caught in the time of the rock. They were everywhere, appearing without forced removal. I carried three or four rocks home, laid them on the heavy shelf without knowing I imitated the institution. Once, building more shelves, I moved several fossils and cut my finger on a piece of wood. Grabbing a towel, I dripped blood on the table, then bandaged it up. Later, placing the rocks where they belonged, I found one with two blood stains that exploded on the dusty surface, clear red lines in perfect, round blossom, dry blood disappearing into the history of stone, dry blood the color of twelve thousand clay bowls.

◆

A Dream

Two men and I stumbled through the vines of the jungle and came to the great cliffs overgrown with the horizon of mountains and valleys, waiting for us to jump over the edge. We sat with our feet dangling miles above the floor of the canyon, dozens of small monkeys appearing behind us. As I turned to watch them, the two men hid their faces in the vines. The three of us sat and waited, each monkey covering itself with huge leaves as they quietly watched us. I turned again and saw the monkey faces were yellow and round, as if cast in golden molds, each one different and hiding an intricate gaze—symbols woven in wonder and despair.

Without seeing his face, I heard one man say the monkeys warned him about the gorilla approaching across the valley floor. If it found us, we had to jump off the edge to save ourselves. I sat and waited, kept looking into the abyss of brown and green, the fear of falling driving me closer to jump. Without warning, the gorilla appeared below, its shoulders and thick arms dangling over the trees. It quickly disappeared before I could study its huge head. The last thing I heard were breaking branches behind us, the monkeys chattering that the gorilla was carrying a heavy rosary made out of flat stones tied to a long vine.

I didn't believe it, until I heard a crashing noise. I turned to see the gorilla a few feet behind me, the rosary dragging along the ground. A second crash surrounded me and entered my legs as I let go. Monkeys were the last thing I saw as I fell, woke up to see their frozen, cast faces staring down at me like bright suns across the deep valley floor.

◆

my hands are dusting the lord
my hands are carving the ground

my hands are opinionated
my hands are escaping

my hands are following the feet
my hands are impossible

my hands are shaking
my hands beat the wind

my hands put out the lights
my hands opened the eyes

my hands ran like beggars
my hands took in the thief

my hands were broken in sadness
my hands were repaired with light

my hands hammered the sun
my hands stayed to the end

my hands won't answer this question
my hands were larger than the last sound

•

I am older than the thorn and the cottonwood.
The eye with dirt waters and can't see me arrive.

I go to the first house and knock and wait, then sleep.
No one answers because I am older than anyone in my town.

I called to myself and woke my wife upon the dirt floors.
No one held me and no one believed I could open my eyes.

When I emerged from the mud and the walls and the rain,
I heard a voice singing about love and the blind hills behind me.

I turned to see people running in the distance and knew I was wrong.
There was no one older than me.

Yet, it was my family fleeing and having to hide from the earth.
When I was older than the lesson, I closed the adobe and left.

The eyes with dry sun and the dream come alive stared at me.
I called myself by a different name and many people loved me.

No one watched me leave, but my family was already beyond reach.
Yes, I am older than the thorn and the cottonwood.

When I displaced them, I had no choice and looked up at the sky for years.
When I allowed them to return, I loved them.

◆

His face was covered by snow.
When he opened his eyes, the white hawk returned.
His face was eaten by worry.
When he sat up, it was the summer of the folded hands.
His face was solemn and kind.
When he stood up, his legs were like trees.
They planted themselves and grew colonies of fire
that seeped into his toes and made him smarter.

His face was covered by snow.
When he loved the terrain, it brought him the wolf
that followed him into the canyon.
His face was eaten by ringing bells and a torn claw.

When he sat up, it was the winter of full baskets,
cracked shoulders, and the skull of the iron man.
His face was round and glowing.
When he stood up, his back hurt but made way
for the weight of the fallen wolf,
the companion who mistook the burning feet
of men for animals that bled salvation.

His face was covered by snow.
When he loved the tree woman, it brought him breasts
and the butter that saved his world.
His face was eaten by hands and tongues and feasts.
When he sat up, it was the spring of gnarled things—
a cooked tumbleweed, a frozen carcass of sparrow,
the folded body of the white owl dying of grief.
When he stood up, his stomach was full.
When the tree woman embraced him with branches,
he waited for the first green buds and never left.

◆

A woman walking slowly in a dark blue coat.
Earrings from love and the desert.
A slight limp from a bad knee.
Medium length brown hair.
Pausing, moving toward the house.
A woman walking slowly in a dark blue coat.
Wearing a Hopi ring with symbols of migration.
A ring with symbols of migration.
Of migration.
Migration.

◆

To touch with dust
is dust
      explanation code
solid fast encirclement
      the word kept
to one side
fought with arrows
      decided against
history its drippings
      To touch
is absolution
      Down the frets
against foreheads
      fastened
to what is loved
caught as butterfly
      windows
amusement besides sorrow
flattered opinionated
      rosaries
opinionated rosaries
crossed kissed kept
      fought over
as if shrouded shoulders
were aliens praying
      for power
scent of apples
scent of candles
      smell
sewed into wishes
absolution code
      against repeating
the same prayer

the familiar caskets
          long awaited
failure folded into
          precious stones
to be worn
between the eyes
          when knees hurt
from kneeling
to a wind held
          prisoner
in-between centuries
taken for granted
          as if black praying
men
are brown kneeling
men
          asking for
the same thing
the same food

♦

broken stick
embedded in the ear
glistens with an oath

finds him waiting
for the feud
to initiate embraces

broken stick
embedded in the heart
to beat a forest

let it spread
to the territory where
he wants to be humming

like a mountain possessed
of praise the narrative
swelling of mirrors blessed

with erasure toward
sitting down relaying
the cost of lasting filaments

broken stick
embedded in the brown skin
found as a blessed piece

of something growing
to replenish what collapsed
when grace was a rattle a stick

◆

He exists for mercy and the vowel of the turtles. He has traveled this far and
has found a reason to believe the infinite movement will be rewarded with the
community. He passes the years and finds simple laws, approaches the water
because it is the water that brings hosts and sounds and the strength to go on.

◆

I Huddle the Impossible River

I huddle the impossible river and let go
Tortilla makers scream at me and let go

Second Shell

Abuelas with torn skirts dance with me and let go
Viejos with broken beer bottles point at me and let go

I huddle the impossible river and come back
Tamale weavers eat and eat and come back
Homeboys with mohawks and Hendrix T-shirts shit on me and come back
Selena look-alike girls show their nipples and come back

I huddle the impossible river and fly
Fathers with rusted Chevys give themselves new tattoos and fly
Mothers with burned hands reshape tortillas and fly
Brothers with Vietnam faces patch their hatred and fly
Sisters with pregnant futures keep my photo and fly

I huddle the impossible river and grow old
I huddle the sacred rosary and forget the words to grow old
I huddle the bitter bread of communion and watch the priest grow old
I huddle the whores across the river who die before they grow old
I huddle the impossible lover who loved me and watched me grow old

Tortuga Borders

Select the spot in the sand.
I can't see because the spotlight is hitting me.
Select the river and its burning water.
I can't see because I fell in.
Try and come up on this side.
I can't see because it is too dark.

◆

Two men crouch near the electric fence.
They are cutting the bales of grass tonight.

Two men touch the wire.
They are cutting the thin bodies tonight.
Two men dig under the fence.
They are sinking rapidly toward the other side.

◆

When the sixteen bodies were found in the railroad boxcar, the heat had bloated them to three times their normal size. They had to use long poles to pry loose the women who had stiffened with their babies clutched in their arms. When the bodies exploded, no one reported how bright and colorful the Rio Grande river glowed in the night.

◆

I almost crossed.
I almost fell in.

I heard the shouts.
I ducked the bullets.

I saw the rape.
I saw the green shirts.

I almost crossed.
I was never caught.

I want to cross.
I want to see.

I want the devil to come out of the water
and take care of the hungry rats.

I want to cross.
I want to work.

I want to talk.
I want to hide.

I want the devil to douse the lights
and let me drown on my own.

◆

The border patrol agent ripped her dress off and fucked her from behind, two
other slick officers holding her down, half-laughing, half-staring at how her

shiny brown ass quivered and leaped as their partner showed them how to do
it with glee.

◆

There was no one there.
No one waited by the irrigation canal.
The gates were closed.
The water was swift and dangerous.

There was no one there.
No one waited for the first man to come across.

◆

The border was closed.

◆

Border exclusion:

This involves taking tons of tortillas,
building stacks of them dozens of feet
above the fence along the border,
forming a real tortilla curtain
for the hungry and the dead.

◆

He convinces the mojados to cross
and carry their border wherever they go.

It is the only way to avoid the patrol cars
and the helicopter insects hovering
over the black walls of two countries.

If you carry the border wherever you go,
it may be a line from the center of your chest,
running down between your nipples
to your belly button,
your stomach dirty with mud from the Rio Grande.
Then, it would be a vertical border
oozing down your chest,
not the horizontal line drawn over the heart
to keep it beating and tame.

◆

They were watching on radar—
     couldn't believe how forty illegals
simply rose off the ground,
     some out of the river,
and flew over the barricades,
     the fence below them untouched
by the wings of flying people
     entering without a place to land.

◆

One night, in the bitter cold of January, one of them knocked at my door. I
rose from sleep, my tiny house one hundred yards from the river. I opened
the door to greet one of them dripping wet and shivering, asking me over and
over for a dry shirt. I motioned to him to wait, went to my closet and found an
old jacket. I brought it to the door and he yanked it out of my hands, thanked
me with a whisper, then took off running under the bending cottonwoods that
fought the wind and the uncontrollable shadows of a moving land.

◆

Signs on the border:

DON'T STOP.

KEEP YOUR HANDS OFF THE FENCE.

DON'T DRINK FROM THE RIVER.

CARRY A ROCK IN BOTH HANDS.

DON'T STOP RUNNING.

WHEN YOU ARE CAUGHT, PLEASE COME BACK.

◆

The reporter went with the border patrol agent one night. The agent asked the reporter, "Have you ever gone Code Three before?" The reporter had not. The siren in the green car went off and they tore down a narrow, desert road some-where east of San Diego. When they got to the canyon, a helicopter was shin-ing a powerful beam over the broken terrain of dirt hills and tumbleweeds. Two border patrol vans sat at the top of one hill. The reporter climbed out in the darkness, the beam from the helicopter giving the only light. The agent had given him a flashlight before disappearing in the night. The reporter thought he spotted him climbing the hill toward the other waiting agents. The hill was thick with huge barrel cactus and thorny ocotillo trees. The helicopter's noise was deafening and made it harder for the reporter to concentrate on where he was going. He didn't know if it was okay to turn on the flashlight. He was about to click it on, when he stumbled over an invisible cactus, felt several thorns cut his legs, and went down. As he landed on his stomach, he tried to roll over and stand up. Out of breath, the reporter sat in the dirt, his legs stinging with cuts. Suddenly, out of nowhere, dozens of moving shadows ap-peared around him. The helicopter beam had not reached them yet. Before he could move out of the way, men and women were running and stumbling over him. The reporter covered his head with his hands as one man tried to kick him in the ribs. The reporter managed to move behind the cactus he had tripped over. This helped. He stood weakly and stared at the sight of at least one hundred illegals running across the hill. All hell broke loose as the helicopter spotted them. The entire area was washed in a brilliant white light. The reporter had to shield his eyes with his hands to keep from being blinded. He heard shouts and screaming people. The helicopter came closer and dust flew everywhere. The reporter opened one eye and watched as several agents ran down the hill trying to arrest as many of the illegals as they could. Before the next ball of dust choked him, the reporter stared at the unbelievable sight of large groups of people all vanishing at once! One second there was chaos as the agents pounced on the running illegals. The next moment, as the helicopter drowned all thought and being, the fleeing people simply vanished into the night. The helicopter rapidly backed off as its beam caught nothing but the stunned agents who stood panting, some of them kneeling, others slowly turning in circles as the crowd they were herding together had simply disappeared into the great mouth of the black canyon, whose opening even the helicopter had not been able to penetrate.

◆

Searching for signs of the green cars,
the gangs of illegals waiting to attack the train
only fifty yards inside this country.

Searching for the holding pens,
the green buses running out of gas,
the holes in the fence never repaired.

Searching for the drainage pipes
giving a clean straight path
from Juarez to westside El Paso
without anyone noticing.

Searching for the thousand caught in May.
Searching for the fifteen hundred in June,
the two thousand in July,
the twenty-eight hundred under the moon of August
when no one returns to their country without forgetting its name.

◆

He stood up to the officer
without backing down.
He defied the man
and got beaten without
a single TV camera in sight.

◆

If I lived there, I remember.
If I walked along the line, I recall.
If I felt threatened, I know.
If I was questioned, I answered.
If I knew where they hid as the cars came,
I only pointed to myself.
If I knew how to run,
I ran.
If I could feed myself,
I went hungry.
If I never lived there,
I knew every street and locked car.
If I was caught twenty-eight different times,
I found a way back.

◆

At the top of conscience is a void.
At the top of the electric fence, pigeons shit, but it doesn't fry.
At the top of the mountain, cameras play their hand.
At the top of the river, the current takes two or three of them today.
At the top of the international bridge, hundreds march and protest without
    knowing
there are fourteen bodies lodged between the concrete pillars of sister cities
waiting for this nightmare to finally end.

◆

The Rio Grande is full.
The Rio Grande is not afraid.

The Rio Grande has been channeled.
The Rio Grande loves its mud.

The Rio Grande is deeper than the deep.
The Rio Grande smells.

The Rio Grande is proud of its history.
The Rio Grande is a river.

The Rio Grande is green.
The Rio Grande is silver.

The Rio Grande smokes.
The Rio Grande peels the skin off bodies.

The Rio Grande shines like a mirror reflecting millions of brown faces.
The Rio Grande is full.

The Rio Grande is empty.

♦

"What time will you cross?"

"Eleven thirty tonight?"

"What time will they start drowning?" ·

"What?"

"What time will they be swept away?"

"What do you mean?"

"Is there only mud?"

"Have you seen all the water in the river?"

"How many will drown?"

"How many do you want in tomorrow's count?"

♦

Silence as they cross.
Silence as deep as the heart.
When the silence is a shout, the lights strike.
When silence is a murmur, all hands are tied behind the back.
Silence was taught at the border.
It was music.
It was wet clothing.
It was leaving some behind, only to find them weeks later in Denver.
It was leaving some behind, only to hear one died in Albuquerque.
It was leaving some behind, never to hear from two sons again.

•

Fifty-thousand dollars per yard. It is costing fifty-thousand dollars per yard to fence in the border from the California end. There is progress along the arroyos, the caves, the long stretches of cracked, concrete channels. The fence will be longer than the Great Wall of China. Prediction: It will reach from the Pacific to the Gulf Coast and belong to everybody who wants to carefully walk up to it and touch the solid steel black bars. Solid Border.

Third Shell

The turtles dropped like rain, covered his desires with the granite of non-movement, a steady approach toward the country of colored walls and the jaws of a biting might. The turtles dropped like rain and he knew it was time to gather what each shell carried, how the silence of the turtles had the instance of music—the sound he was warned about long ago. The turtles moved beyond reach, their sudden migration surprising him, making him see how several years had already happened and he was not quite ready to sing. The turtles reappeared to sustain the present. Several of them fell out of his hair. A few clung to his back and changed it into a lake where no fish dwelled. One small turtle even carved a blind leg upon the surface of his mind. It is why he is beginning to accept the answer is the only mouth that can swallow whole bodies. The turtles dropped like rain out of a sky that rarely forgives what it can't see. He assumed he walked in the right direction, but their falling could not be verified by his moving feet. In the world of turtle words, a locomotive went by. It was painted green and was headed for the coast. He was given a glass of water as he stood on top of a canyon and watched the train move in the distance. As he stared at the horizon, he pictured a small boy in a field, holding the string of a kite, the colorful box thing having broken from the string moments before—its tiny form slowly disappearing against the blue shoulders of a sky that had quit raining turtles and was now prepared to let him live.

◆

flies, midgets,
horns, clouds,
thieves, windows,
iron gates, cows,
shoes, cars,
combs, teeth,
baskets, brooms,
owls, perfume,
monks, legs,
revolutions, sparkplugs,
cats, eyeglasses,
tongues

◆

The Blackfoot Flute Man

after a Bodmer painting

His face, painted red, streaks tears into white lines transforming color, moving it to a farther shore of bone, grimace and stare that shows who he was when the strangers sailed up the river, why they etched him onto the canvas to forget the genocide. His flute is the pipe of wood some men grip in their dying hands, the earlier day when they discovered silence was the sex of the earth. It was music from the mouth that pushed the mountains closer, voices spreading their arms to the notes. His flute started the fire above his winter coat to return the buffalo into the shadows of his long hair, the coat draped over shoulders of the last flute blower.

People want me to explain what happened to the poem inside my shirt, the violin of corn my family willed me, guitar of redwood lying on my marriage bed. They want to know what became of the man hidden in the tree, formed by fingers carving the longest flute, instrument hiding in the bark for an old man to find. His mother told him he wore a birthmark on his lips, hidden when he touched them to the flute of water, stepping into the tide where the musician hunted as a boy. He searched for his first flute in the mass of dying prey, the bone of song covering his mouth in blood.

He unbraids his hair, wonders why the face of his wife is painted completely green, why it doesn't match the red smeared on his face. She approaches him with her low song, breath of flute she taught him, the shape he once carved into her naked body. He folds his arms around the flute and repeats the words of one father, "The mouth moves to destroy the song. The throat rises to give it birth." The flute man turns his back to the light and raises the wood to his lips, red paint on his face forming a new profile, a hard way of learning to play the second instrument invented across the rolling hills.

◆

Wherever he goes,
he feels everyone watches him.
He has not told anyone how it must end,
how the search for the circle must be granted
before the century ends and tireless cars take away
the final chance to clear the river.

A thousand waves.
His grandmother.
A thousand currents.
His grandfather.
He doesn't know how he got this.
They will come for him.
They will be gentle and let him know.
A thousand hands.
The earth allows the reptile.
The earth allows the amphibian.
The earth allows cold blood.

The earth said it was only a story
where the family evolved close to the ground,
in order to prosper and survive.

•

Inside the symbol, the boy gains.
Inside the window, the boy stares.
Inside the window, the animal behaves.
Inside the window, the praying one prays.
Inside the window, there is no shame.
Inside the window, the boy stays.
Inside the window, the water sways.
Inside the window, the boy relays.
Inside the window, the animal contains.
Inside the window, the praying one cares.
Inside the window, there is time.

•

Killer Bees

Everything is composed of unwanted fire like the young boy killed by the bees in the southern part of the state, their fury hurtling the boy toward the honeyed halls of family whispers where they speak of how he danced in death like a flower gaining speed from the addiction to the sting. Everything is opposed to its use by the migration of bees, how they appear near us to sign our faces, sing of a happy tone when the tiniest things change the elevator of nature, drop us too deeply behind the days when we were supposed to die. The terrible bees and the honey are the only love we leave for the humidity, the staff, anger of wings. Everything decomposes as it drips down the trunks of the saturated trees, huge hives vibrating as sticky hearts buried in our heaving chests, flat waters shimmering above the fields where we lie waiting for

untamed migrations, movements that cut our faces, fresh rivers of pollination
where we swell up and don't even scream.

◆

"Knowledge, however, is elsewhere."
—Charles Wright

I think someone will tell me it is time
to enter the new century.

I will not understand where we have been.
The boy mistreats his dog and is punished years later.

Someone will buy me a cup of coffee.
I will drink it and think of Pancho Villa
breaking into my grandfather's house,
looking for the guns and bullets,

finding the glowing lantern instead.
Someone will play their guitar at the funeral.

Two small boys will run away and never be found.
I will not confess I saw them crossing the street.

I will be too busy striking a match.
I think I can wait until the century ends.

I have no reason to start my fortune
by telling a story that has no ending.

◆

We talked about the children crying along the river, the border running away with the people, stealing them toward the night of the flood. I had a dream where a black and white photo appeared—a close-up of what a voice called "the rabies"—an actual form of mad hysteria. In the dream, the rabies were not a disease, but took the shape of two dog-like creatures. They were half-tree, half-animal, black shiny bodies embedded in the trunk of the tree. They had wooden limbs for arms and legs, roots growing out of their snouts, their barks petrified into the tree. It was my vision of "rabies"—I didn't know why it came after we talked about the children drowning in the river, crossing illegally from Mexico. I wanted to find out without guilt. I had to go home knowing the children had not turned into the rabid tree dogs who growled and spit at me without being able to move or extract themselves from the tree. When I woke, I walked along the river to search for things I left there—objects I tossed into the water years ago, surrounded myself with the quiet sobs of children I had never met and could never allow into my dreams again.

♦

I go out beyond the safest light and fill my stomach with the last tortilla I ate before I realized I was feeding the wrong cause—swallowing the vowel hidden in the language I never learned until I was five years old. Before that, the sound of Spanish confusion filled my ears and made me hide in the closet when my father came home looking for me. I hid under the bed one time because I had done something wrong. He came into the house slipping his belt off his waist, calling for me. I hid in the darkness and knew the words he spoke in English. I wanted to cry in a different language, run into the light and tell my father I had done nothing wrong.

I go out to watch the morning stabs of yellow air and know they are remains of hunger the world could not swallow, breathing air from the past following me. I stared at the fresh green arms of the caraganda—the moist trails of tortillas I ate the day I could finally speak English. My grandmother watched me as if I was no longer the boy she raised, feeding me too many tortillas to keep me quiet, these flowing branches of caraganda covering the colors I could not repeat in English—mistaking the word for red with the word for green in the first grade—white for black, yellow for the brown mounds of tortillas left alone on the table when the voices pushed me away.

◆

My sorrow embedded
I ask myself to quit believing
Along displays of skeletons
Embedded for historical study
My sorrow moving
I ask myself to learn
Beside displays of masks
Tombs where nomads dance
My sorrow dominating
That tone of voice singing
Wondering why honey drips
Slowly into my cupped hands.

◆

I Am Walking Inside a Joseph Cornell Box

I am walking inside a Joseph Cornell box and the plastic dolls and watches and the mighty birds are in my way. I keep walking and my entire kitchen is inside the box. When I pause to open the refrigerator, a small boy comes out of it with a bag of carrots in his hand. I am walking inside the past and can't follow this child. When I look through the glass cover on the box, there is no one looking in. Suddenly, the dust of old glue is in my nose and I see a man walking through the deep snow, the recurring sight of the woman who surprised me by disappearing around the corner of the box. I am walking inside brilliance that has nothing to do with the confined space of this wooden box, the old magazine articles pasted along the sides, fading print reading "to determine the rate of heartbeat, take one spoon of . . ." I am walking inside movement in the large room, display lights setting the future for me, but the beams can't find me because I am huddled behind a tiny stone turtle Cornell mounted in the right corner. I hide behind the green shell of the turtle and wait for water to start dripping, the answer to my escape petrified inside this miniature creature, whose four spread legs and dark shell can hardly be seen by anyone who looks in. I am walking inside a Cornell box, but the car that almost hit me doesn't stop as I quickly run across the street and pick up the receiver on the pay phone that has been ringing and ringing.

◆

I have a name for myself.
I have motion and the wisdom of calibers.
I found two cucumbers growing in the garden,
left them there to go back to earth.
I have a name for myself.
It lingers with the dark stories of love,
how my name was taken by her departure.
I found I was still here when she left.
I had two ways of dying—one was to hang
on the wall in an intricate painting.
The second was to keep talking
to stay awake, diminish the pain of
reverberation, allow fresh emergence
from a thick cottonwood tree,
its thick, gray bark splitting open
as a man walks out of it.
I have a name.
I found the river does nothing to me,
the flat clouds above it dancing to warn me,
the mist below it deciphering windows,
brushing them with a message of warning,
the mountains I have wanted to ignore returning
to erode their brown waves into the soft closing of my eyes,

the dangers of acoustic guitars swallowing romance,
the fire in the knuckles healing after two or three days,
a hair of twisted gray falling between my eyes after years
of trying to grow it long without anyone saying it is wrong
to look the way I should have looked—
to have spoken what I always knew,
the mountains I have wanted to forget raining
up there to brush syllables out of memory.

◆

I speak to the voice that left me years ago.
It is water entering the hair of someone being born.
I speak to the voice that came back by design
and a few bright candles.
It is the borderline between instruction
and giving away what we have forgotten.

◆

Remember Rexroth telling the train workers to lie down
and die for what they believe in.
Recall James Wright weeping in front of a tree
where a silent owl peers down at him.
Don't forget Hugo knocking on the door
of the wrong tavern, wondering why
the bottles blinded him with their furious light.

◆

I was here before.
I know this place where love calls the broken

Third Shell

Here is where the hand is forgiven
Here is where the loud heartbeat is a pantomime

Here is where smooth arrows involve opening the heavens
There is where the first turtle landed and laid its eggs

Back in the desert stone a child slaps your face
Back in the desert stone a child spits in your face

Back in the mountain hole a child condemns your fate
Back in the mountain star a child loves you and waits

◆

When there is time, he rises like a priest and asks the tunnels to repeat what
he has just said. This involves cutting pieces of bread into glowing mounds of
sustenance no one foreshadowed or believed could exist.

◆

Back in the room the draped woman designs your fate
Back in the room the black widow moves slightly

Back in the room the light appears then fades
Back in the room the silence scares you

Back in the room the black widow devours the male
Back in the room the white ball hangs in the air

Back in the room the draped woman undresses
Back in the room the silence turns to magic

◆

A tiny man with a long, brown beard plays the sitar and wonders why there are several dozen sparrows falling out of the sky, bouncing on the ground around his feet, a few feathers floating in the air to bend themselves around the sharp notes of instruments.

•

what if I was afraid
what if I had no choice but to fold my hands together
and ask a burned saint for some kind of forgiveness
would I be punished for changing the name of the statue
would anyone care or would they let me repeat what happened

•

Gray, allow me. Blue, take the long hair from my wish. When the song enters, I escape from the grip of color. Store the brushes in your blood. Paint when the music allows you. In the storm, a hawk flies blind. In the clearing, a hawk flies blind. We both removed its eyes with water. We had to close its vision so we could love. Yellow, the corn is family. Brown, the skin is burned. When the machine is only a rake, clear the rocks from the garden. When the arms are only bones, tear the stalks from the vegetables. Red, as if the flesh cares. Green, what is left for punishment. The hoe of desire leans on the wall. Legs and arms and seeds. Months of oleanders. When I welcome their growth, too close. This can be the answer. What did you believe I was telling you when the star fell across the desert and I only saw it when I was twenty-one? How do you condemn men who have only seen it once? Since the spade is buried in mud, the toads grow larger. Since I have no more seeds, the soil enriches its own shadow. Junction of exact morning. Quick start for the parting sky. Keep one less amphibian for exhaustion. Brush the purple wasp with its own black stinger. The first person who showed me how to plant was going to forgive me. The second person who nourished me knew it had to do with some kind of harvest. Since they gave me a chance, I can't expand the yards of grass. Since I am watering the black mud, I see several faces buried in it. Since I am going to dig with my bare hands, my senses have been crushed with all the blooming. Smell of herbs, sperm-tailed stems, womb-green-wet-intentional undergrowth—Weeks away from memory. Days from having to memorize how tall everything grew. Months from clearing the mud to stand up as one man who found out the bright skulls of love and hate must be planted so the past can have a garden to dry its itching pollen, a place torn out of the thick grass that has no body.

•

I lived there twenty-five years
I had nothing else to say
my silence was simple and unattached
I left before the river became a simple line in the dirt

•

caskets thongs slippers T-shirts shields flowers candles wax from the ears of an old man mustard jalapeños percussion books discs salt fountains car tires dry autumn leaves wet autumn leaves cymbals corn on the cob frozen chicken breast check book barefeet toothpaste cats sweaters hiking boots condoms wooden legs garbanzo beans torn magazines headlights combs shoelaces paper clips diet cokes pumpkin pie guitar strings sleeping cats black widows centipedes a fat cardinal nickels dimes postage stamps

•

when you fast on the twig your father behaves like a dreaded angel of glass
when you fast on the rosary your mother behaves like a dreaded angel of
    hair
when you fast on the paper your voice behaves like a dreaded angel of lies
when you fast on the water your feet behave like a dreaded angel with
    power

◆

You imagine your true home is a metal chamber made of flowers, seashells, and the images of lost lovers who loved you and gave you time to heal. You imagine they, too, are inside metal chambers whose walls throb with desire, but won't let them out to see you at your best, least worrisome, and most confident period of your life.

◆

He started playing the mud on his fingers
He began to taste the grains of sand
He wanted to smear it on the belly of a devil cactus
He needed to learn about the green face of the wind
He started playing the mud on his fingers
He ended the song by washing his hands
He stopped moving his thumbs to the long rings of sound
He sat down and bowed his head and gave in to the mud

◆

Creation was a woman who wouldn't come near me. I love to draw pictures of odd things in black and white, intricate misspellings that teach me a language for the eye. Misguided missile about the blossom in the navel. Fortune teller asking for your palm.

Condition — addition — shining complex animal forgotten in the history of animals bred to follow one master into the storm of tumbleweeds fixed to his hair. What became of the spinning form dividing the fingernail into broken shards of pottery touched by the human hair of the animal?

As if this is the prophet eating beans and tortillas. As if I could save him and give him back his name. As if I could show him how to fix his moment of making, so it will make him a part of the swaying of what he missed.

Third Shell

I loved the calendars of sleep and the lies I told my younger sisters. I told them there was a ghost hiding in the closet, but I did not have the courage to open it when we turned off the lights and pretended I was the brother that would save them, let them live their own lives when I left.

One morning, I wake with photos of the hostages. They have been dead my entire life. I bring them back to speak to me, let me know where my poor ancestors came from, what rancho they worked on—where I could find their graves and stop thinking about the dead. One morning, my big toe hurts with the buried seed of the working man—my uncle I never knew who gave me his feet so I could walk away from the truth, send him a message in an oversized shoe and encourage him to bring me a crimson robe—an ash for the forehead— his old army uniform and the sword with jagged edge where he cut off the Japanese head. One morning, I become a snowy yard—a cottonwood full of moss—a cicada changing sound—moldy bread on the ground—watermelon seeds—stinking rinds—a crazy flame from a village boy who burned down the only movie house in the damned town. I sit down to a fried egg, my abuela frying it so I can quit crying and go play outside as fast as I can, the boys next door waiting to beat me up as I come out with a full stomach and a baseball bat.

Creation is a woman singing to me with her broken acoustic guitar, the paint on her lips glistening like the light that misspelled my name before I ever existed in her heart. Creation is the hammer underneath her navel pressing the man who loves her and gives her another chance. They would do well to leave you alone, let you trace the arms of the forgiver into a magnificent creation meant to be translated by tongueless fish and tired monks who return from their graves in the walls of ivory to listen to what you have been trying to say to the world, yet the world refuses to see you because it does not acknowledge walls.

◆

picking the sorrow out of the eyes
placing it inside the palm of the hand

the designated dancer is supposed to tap me on the shoulder and wait
the painted widow is supposed to write me a letter

the angry politician is supposed to vote for me instead of himself
the only side of the story belongs in strange museums

the forsaken arm of the stone
it was mine at all times

what I wanted was repeated
it gave me design for a secret

to live within the recognition of doubt and loss
can be the loudest whisper trapped in a room

mounds of faces as if love mattered
mounds of faces as if love brought us back

rising knees capturing the stone to give speed to desire
causing the trembling shadow to emerge and be believed

cars flashing by as if the two frames fit together
before they are taken apart by the wind

two films adjoining the star demanding one system open its mouth
two forests merging before the last country tears them down

opens its mouth
closes its umbilical cord

◆

One lone horseman believes the road is turning yellow and wants to dismount and touch the ground to make sure he is riding in the direction his grandfather told him to go.

•

Weldon Kees Crosses the Street in El Paso

No one knows he came down here, his clothes still wet from the bay. He hid on Paisano Street for a few months, the south El Paso whores tattooing his heart with the shaved head of a roadrunner—that fast animal that appeared to Kees as he stepped off the train. The bird disappeared behind a mound of tumbleweeds as the poet took his coat off and held his face to the heat. When he opened his eyes, he thought he saw the image of Pancho Villa crossing the street. When Kees followed, he got lost in the mercado, baskets of avocados and grapefruit waiting for his hunger. Kees swept the floors of my old high school, ten years before I set foot there. I knew it was him when I found an old yearbook, photos of the janitors included every year. There he was—poet of the empty desk and the gulls of the bridge. Kees in El Paso. Even his face and moustache were the same. A few days before he left the desert for good, he was walking along the Rio Grande when a bright light hit a cottonwood tree half a mile downriver. Kees blinked and saw the tree in flames. He didn't think it could be true and did not notify anyone, but turned and walked back to town. At the train station, on the way to San Antonio, he spotted the headlines in the paper—Fire Burns Miles of Mesilla Valley. He put the paper down without reading, the wide brimmed hat covering his closed eyes, the sound of gulls waving white bodies over large waves of scorched water.

•

caught with flowers in my hand
let go before I bow in shame

caught with an astrid lime wish
caught with a burned tooth

caught with the slowing piano reciting vowels
let go to ease the echo and step on the road

caught with anger doubt moisture seeping from the dream
finger of glass embedded in the ear to grant sound and life

caught with winter demanding eighteen notes from the tree
the tree shifting to hear how composition demeans opposition

caught despite the freedom to impress a few situated chambers
basking in the thumb gift of imported hollowed out faith

caught between the rolling level of salad bread soup danger
settling down into the valley to wait for the rock carving to sing

•

it was imagination forested in a cup of onions crying to sing
how the lone man knows what lies ahead and what stays ahead of him

it was freedom denied freedom allowed freedom bestowed again
no one could cry and stay in the same place without leaving smoke

it was simply a slow way of loving someone else and being loved
basking in the thumb gift of exported fire spelling its own name

•

He imagined what it was like to move under the blanket and find the different
colored paints melting on the sheets. He imagined what it was like to paint
her body with his hands, smear the symbols between her breasts so she could

see he still loved her. He imagined what it was like to see colors in the dark, to see how they changed when the morning light came and dried his paint into hard profiles.

•

it could have ended at the edge of the canyon
it ended at the edge of the outstretched hand instead

it could have extended to the end of the century
it fell short of the black cliff and created two new worlds

it could have bitten the soul into fourteen pieces to spice the tongue
when it was discovered a wall of love vibrated in its place

it could have mended the wall of vines and encircled the knees
it pushed hunger into the mouth and fed the child for years

it could have created music to fly swans beyond capture and cages
it let them go free and painted itself as a life saving force

it could have unfolded into tiny wishes tempting the brain to grow
it kept silent instead

•

The carved god did not believe in peace. He shook himself. It was time to make sense of all this, but too many of his people had left, changed into other cultures that had nothing to do with his desire for peace, for the land, for the true moment of kneeling and sweating under the running tears on the statue of La Virgen de Guadalupe. The carved god did not believe in this kind of peace and it was something hard for him to accept. He stepped out into the street and headed toward the river.

◆

It must have been the trees I noticed one day when I stepped out of the cloud and no longer looked back. They were bare trees, dark and falling, as if some invisible hand could hold them up for me to see, the matador swinging the red cape three times, his thighs brushing the bull as if the crowd already had blood on its mind, the matador switching globes of sweat for the will to live and swing and swing, spinning in the dirt to disappear into the only bullfight I ever attended as a young boy, the smell of excited men in the packed stadium making me feel as if the world of men was the scene where the bull went down to its knees, crashing through the dirt to come out on the other side of the earth as a folded and neatly packed cube of muscle, blood, and the only day I have not recalled in the millions of moments when I hated everyone around me.

◆

The sensitive, bald man bowed down to pray and hate the broken sticks.

◆

No one took it away
It has no cause nor grief

It sounds like bells rolling down to design laughter
Voices of men echo behind the walls yearning

No one placed it in the flame of the candle
It emerged and became a sudden cry that fell to the floor

It has no color and has never heard the word "religion"
No one opened the book to the melting sentence

It was only a closed book lying there assuming the morning
When everyone saw what it was, they became themselves.

◆

Baskets of startled hands, broken elbows raising their energy to the sun, withering back down to be replaced by strong children who have memorized oaths and songs that are not going to be forgotten. Baskets of startled hands shaking when the earthquake passes beyond their lives and becomes something else in the history of loss.

◆

No it is not.
Yes, it is going to be.

No, it does not commission greed.
Yes, it behaves as if it wished to be.

After you are gone,
the moths start to fly.

After you are gone,
the moths burn.

After you are gone,
the light bulbs shatter.

After you are gone,
the highways burn.

After you are gone,
the moths spell names.

After you are gone,
the moths are born.

After you are gone,
the purple stems break.

◆

Sometimes you are naked and the floss on your skin becomes a gold shield that entrails and wraps your heart in the petals of a windy desire, as if the sending forth of the tribe meant you were going to be worshipped and forgiven for having told a tale that changed the dreams of those around you. Sometimes you are naked and there is no one there to help you put your clean, brittle clothes back on without sending a prayer into the water for you and anyone that looks like you.

◆

He came back to ask for more.
    He had no money.
He ate out of empty bowls.
    He asked for little.
He came back to talk.
    He asked for the turtle.
He opened his eyes.
    He was the turtle all along.
He came back and asked for more.
    He had rice.
He drank out of clay bowls.
    He came back to speak.

◆

Burying the Toad

It came out from under the root of the old cottonwood, a fat yellow toad with its front leg missing, my attempts to dig up the dead root invading its home. It leaped into the grass and lay still, jumped one more time before dying. All I did was cut the rotting tentacle of the tree, but the toad died under my shovel. I dug a small grave in the garden, dropped the toad and covered it with mulch. The next day I was surprised at the white maggots coming out of the soil, surprised it did not take long to erase what I had done. Burying the toad means there are blind voices bleeding through the earth. Accidentally killing the sleeping toad shows me there is something under the will to make things grow. Its missing right arm was left underground, sliced by my shovel as I pulled the thick root to expose a vein of copper stretching across the yard. Burying the toad created food for the white worms of death. Did they take it all, or will my garden change from hidden remains of the toad? Is it the wrong place to nourish what we can't foresee will take place? What we are named for has something to do with burying the toad. What I am looking for in watering my plants has something to do with its missing arm, its bloated, yellow skin, its way of staring at me as it trembled and died.

◆

Light green flaps that extend to the sky, allowing their enormous white blossoms to shoot between the helix and the strange air of the magnolia. Layer upon layer of crowded leaves become seizure and surface tension, the wind blowing gently to spread the odor of magnolia across the square. Searching for the hidden symbol in the painting, there is the falling into that belongs in a story that was never written, a forest where only two magnolias grew — the one planted by the escaped convict who managed to live alone for several years, until they captured him with dry magnolia leaves in his hair — the second tree a gift from a man who didn't know what to mourn — his hands, his parents, or the bare ground where something died. The lone magnolia shifts into the lime-green light of a mistaken interpretation. When the wind stops and the leaves remain as oval memories of things that don't move, the tree stands forever and gets all the water it needs.

◆

When the gleaming man extends his flame,
there is no substitute for transition.
Inspired by the flame of the ancient arrow,
he counts the blossoms of the world.

When the gleaming arm folds and holds paper,
garbage leaves the mind,
trimming the brain into weasels that burrow
beyond the territory—encased in the documents
borrowed when the man thought he was hungry.

When the gleaming boy looks over his shoulder,
a part of the story is done.
Masterful shouts—conditions of absolution—cries and hand signals
creating the cylinder that takes the street—fresh bulbs marking
the brown back as the map where boys danced,
calling to their mothers to take off their clothes—
birth—early age—shame-whispers leading toward
the creation of the gleaming man.

◆

Think of the green stem as a necklace.
        The light that kills desire does not belong.
The black cricket in the mouth of the cat.
        A blind boy defeating the neighborhood.
Think of a solution that suffers ten billion cells.
        Find the doves that tremble on the fence.
Ask the old couple walking by—
The way they worship the light,
        the way they improvise.
The way they thank the world
        for the lines on their hands,

roads and mouths singing
      for what won't arrive.
The manner of walking by the doves
      without startling them into flight.

Think of love as a lyric moment of practice.
      The sense of absent time does not heal.
The needles in the red tree equal darkness.
      A man is finally able to talk to his father.
Think of faith as the distance between whispers and stones.
      Take a kiss on the cheek and say Amen.
The first warning weeps desire into folded hands
      without making you lift your eyes to see.

The way you spin crushed herbs into the air,
      the way it creates an odor.
The way you look like yourself everyday,
      sleep and her name singing
for what has never left you.
      The way of getting up by the water
without looking for rescue or myth.

•

I swat the fly and miss. There are pontifications we are supposed to acknowl-
edge and respect. The woman I love was gone for over a year. She lived on the
other side of the world, then came back. The fly passes my head and lands on
my knee. Since I am wearing shorts, this tickles. It moves before I can reach
for the swatter again. There are highways where my alcoholic friend used to
thumb rides. I have not seen him in years, but I remember he was good at swat-
ting flies. I used to go to his house to watch TV together, and he was always
sitting on his couch with a fly swatter in his hand. We used to watch football on
Sundays and he would swat the sofa in glee after his team scored a touchdown.
Every time I visited, there were at least seven or eight dead flies on the floor

near his feet. I used to count them, but I never asked. They would congregate on his window screens. The few that got in must have loved football. There are sounds in the air we should acknowledge. The fly keeps landing on my bare knees. When Juan Ponce de León tried to conquer Florida in 1521, an arrow pierced his heart. His men carried him back to their ship without exchanging a word with each other. They just stared and stared at their dead leader who had promised them all so much. I think of this after the endless number of mosquitoes I encounter on my summer evening walks. They are not flies, but biting mosquitoes. I think of Juan, go home to scratch my latest bites, and hear something near my head. The same fly has been trapped in my office all day. I grab the swatter and actually kill it on the first try. It lands on the carpet and I think of my old friend. As I pick up the dead thing with the tip of the swatter, I recall I found a bent, twisted swatter in his trashcan the last time I ever saw him. I walked into his living room and he sat glued to the television, a brand new swatter fluttering like a butterfly in his hands.

◆

Every night he stares at the crosses
licking the child's face.
The heart of the stable pounds the family
as deeply as his ability to dance.

Moving his collection of saints from house to house,
he finds cobwebs among the robes and auras.
He places a bottle of green flame by his bed,
waits for the kneeling woman to bless him.

Every night he hangs like a bat,
his long hair smoothing the floor like tall grass.
The heart of the stable is inside the hanging man,
who waits for someone to cut him down for love.

By the door, there is a yellowed piece of paper—
a letter that brought him to the town.
The heart of the stable settles in his chest
as quickly as he takes the woman and drowns.

He hears her dreams and sees the invasion,
how they came for her and gave her a new name.
When they both wake, there are fresh candles
crying brightly on both sides of the bed.

◆

cast of motion out of the vesper dangling down toward the vine pulled against
wild choice retribution escape awareness of toy guest and hallway system de-
rived from lying to the dog unusual beauty causes the itch in the saddle of the
legs that reached the installation first. were there three or four legs rubbing
together? was there a cycle missed from square to circle? broken ribs broken
man broken woman broken boy inside the thumb. could you believe it? can
the hoof prosper? would it matter? did the lettuce hang from the bell feeding
the injured child? did the rain behave as if the world had already ended? de-
cide if the corner where you live belongs desperate cut back into fish history
approach faster than the bleeding desire found years ago hidden from copu-
lating marbles when you first believed in the animal that blessed you missed
you when it was time to blink and steal four fingers from the affronted man
love the morning after the four fingers rubbed in oil to spell hell the morning
taught you to look at each circle growing under each wet eye demanding you
consider it for the first throne of laughter positioned between the legs and the
calling myth when you see it you will know and not ask to be given an explana-
tion a risk a rabid bat a token bone of departed fissures when the temperament
arrives it takes off when music endangers itself there is no control. wombs be-
long to strangers that never loved me don't stop me I can't spell the excitement
trapped in the wall by the mural of the first fish eaten by a naked man and
woman who came here to save the tiny bones of the spine they carry between

their bare toes against the moon is a dish of seeds I couldn't reach without lying to my mother hated her when she censored photos of naked women in ads of the LA Free Press I subscribed to in high school used her black crayon to hide what she didn't want me to see it was dangerous to be influenced by the naked breast the nipple the surge the lift the eye focusing on what flesh spells what flesh bleeds what flesh becomes when it dances behind the black lines of the mother crayon the closed bleep the open sore the power to remove the balls of desire from the balls of growing into the successful collector of breasts who never had to dig through the streaks of black crayon that kept him from frying lying dying defying devouring what enables him to speak.

◆

Goloxina

goloxina—the power of black hair

The great man with long hair and red bandanna knew what we wanted.
He reshaped his cars and women to fit the streets.

He opened his pants and a purple tower rose into the sky.
He closed his pants and people talked about him quietly.

The great man with long hair cut it off and approached me.
He cornered me against the adobe and told me to lick the wall.

He pushed me against the clay and I saw Dios dancing.
He told me not to follow him because women waited.

The great man with long hair was now shaved and bald.
He held his head in his hands and held it up to the moon.

He trembled as people of the 'hood gathered to watch.
He trembled and let go of his head.

It exploded into green, red and white streamers
that flew around the heads of the frozen crowd.

His head generated into colored balls, popcorn and beads
that pelted the people who couldn't move.

When his head was done bursting, the people were a new color.
The headless man gripped his bandanna as he was devoured

by every man, woman, and child whose rainbow hair
had always been longer than the hair of the great man.

◆

A.D.

The new dimension is a throat surviving the cost of stepping into the new
style of century—outside settings tell us no one was kicked out of the calendar.
Even the Aztecs laid down their tools, stared at the great stone wheels when
they rolled out of the picture—the new dimension spits into the wind, carries
a snap of rabbit and the lone commission found in the pocket of the king—
how you carry this dilemma, its alternatives soaking in sunlight, leaving the
small junction clean whistle setting the house down, until it implodes into the
kneeling saint you avoided since the pockets fell out of the river—a new di-
mension beats the clouds in asking for a chance to begin something—even a
dish at the edge of the canyon was enough for eight Anasazi skeletons to disin-
tegrate after seven hundred years—the opening in the plot means this stance
will no longer do—deposits against planning, against the body—when this
new dimension is laughed at, laughing pleases the evidence and settles it be-
yond the house, across the trees where destruction is everything—screened to
be aloof—a path inside the mountain more valuable than this—your lowered
head letting the horns lead the way into the rocks.

◆

Earthworms

I knew the earthworms when I was ill.
Found hundreds of them in the sticky clay
of the backyard.
I dug and dug and planted flowers, shrubs,
new plants to feed the earthworms
that crawled constantly toward me.
I knew the earthworms and I was there.
When I lifted a handful of them,
they weaved through my fingers and fed me.
When I smeared the mud on my pants,
they glowed with the kiss of the earthworm.

I knew the earthworms when I used my shovel
to search for a deeper hole,
opening the ground for earthworm escape.
I filled the holes with new life, plants
to raise myself and be proud that I kept
my head above the swimming clay
of the earthworms that surrounded my knees
and tried to get away from the man coming through.

•

Mano Nova

mano nova—the strongest hand

Mano nova.
Mano şangrada.
   This is how you wear your shirt tonight.

Third Shell

Mano two hands held.
Mano reaching out to wish.
   The avocados are turning purple on the stove.

Mano gripping hope like a fish.
Mano praised for bone and sweetness.
   The green balls of a million birds are shot down by the sky.

Mano nova.
Mano time.
   This is the man waiting for romance to fly out of his radio.

Mano washed in holy water.
Mano painted like a seashell.
   The woman undresses on the outskirts of town.

Mano holding many things.
Mano reaching the barrier of the sun.
   The last man to cross mistook his vegetables for the flat horizon.

Mano desired to lift the stream.
Mano nova.
   This is a shudder even the night moth avoids.

Mano star.
Mano smile without letting go of a single finger.
   The man extends his palm to shake your hand.

◆

Frijole Archive

I try to think of history—
the lacquered cry of a stolen bean.

When I think of the past,
railroads barge into the dream of pots—
burning smells of frijoles,

the anguish of a hungry man
wanting to be seen eating by the fire.

◆

So often, I look up and search
for what is not there.
I think it is about to be and wait.
When it does not appear,
I am in the wrong world, thinking
the amphibian has already crossed the stream.

Year of the Tortuga Egg

True

Green arms of a long banded thing—perhaps fish or reptile coming across the water to find me hiding among black and red vines. Yellow eyes of flowers vibrating with tiny orange flies that look like miniature starfish. When the thing arrives, it shakes itself and comes out of the water. I lean back and don't know how to be afraid. Blue circles of plastic float across the trees, some of them popping in mid-air as if they were never there, one of them passing a few inches from my sweating head. The new creature looks like someone has never loved it, but I can't describe its shape. It still does not see me and I dare not move, the chance to make history attractive and pure. Suddenly, its tail rises in the air and its triangular head points right at me. Its two eyes are like motorcycle wheels spinning out of control. It opens its tiny mouth and recites poems I knew years ago, some lines about being lost and hating the world, stanzas meant for those who hurt me and had no reason to come out on top. This thing makes a deep growling noise that changes the course of the river. As I start to run, it explodes into a million pieces, the idea of it coming apart sending me across the canopy of trees that have hidden me well. Fragments of shiny, intricate skin rain down from the sky, the creature getting the last laugh because I am covered with sharp pieces of electric life that start to buzz, pop, and become a part of me—giving me one chance to learn the code, one try at responding with my own highly charged circuits that will get me there before anything else comes apart.

◆

The turtle monument was glowing when the century died.
It was visited by a number of men who crossed the white sand,
leveled themselves against the sun and entered.

When they heard music, it was erasing the past.
When they saw love, it was gathering the past.

The turtle monument was taken without a fight.

It is the right time for hallucinations.

It is proper to go back to the egg without a fight.

◆

Out of nowhere, he capsizes,
falls into the branch of the tree and goes through the tunnel.
He comes out on the other side of the ocotillo.
He swears he went through the barrel cactus.
He knows he was changed inside the beehive.
Out of nowhere, he capsizes,
finds clues in the blades of the telephone
he finds in the middle of nowhere.

◆

The nest is gone, shell empty.
Someone lifted the eggs and ran.
Someone prospered and told stories.
It had to do with his secrets, his shame,
his manner of knowing what moved over the sand.

◆

His language departs.
He drowns in a brilliant dream of water.
He first came up when the old women spoke.
He was only an idea and one woman drank a green liquid.
He was born.
He was never told you don't throw away
what is taught to you in the world of whispers.

His massacre rises with the moon.
It was told to him when he nested in her belly.
The family was destroyed.
Shells lay everywhere.
Heads were hidden inside.
Scorched shells outnumbered the sun.
He had to start somewhere.

◆

A man inside his shell can't go to his god.

◆

A man crawling to find truth leaves tracks in the mud.

◆

Let him live in the dream of the turtles, so history can begin.

◆

He says, "the origin of water is the origin of the clawed mind."

◆

There is the coast and there is the desert. They were there all along.

◆

The white turtle met the red turtle.
It was too late.
It was too early.
They were both the same.

He sees flowers and loves.
He is about to begin.
He reads the signs with his hands.
He listens to the well.
Once, he swam down there, long ago
before the invention of the truth.
He sweats and runs his fingers
through the drops of sweat.
He memorizes his vision of the nest.
He sees flowers and loves.
He is about to begin.

The same hand that pauses
in the Chihuahua sky
runs its knuckles over the wind
spinning above the Sonora.
A great desert turtle bites down
on the ocean hand.
Streams of flowers and papers
pour out of him.
He was fed breakfast before this.
The same hand that crosses
his heart is found by archaeologists

one hundred years from now.
One of them knew about the species.
One of them loved extinction
in the race of brown men wanting
their entire lifetimes to have
been green.

◆

Miracles Inside the Picture Frame

I believe in the moving visions and the hidden messages, the collection of calendar saints, rosaries, and statues from old churches. I believe in the framed pictures of La Virgen de Guadalupe my grandmother collected for ninety years, the one that moved by itself inside the frame without anyone touching it. She told me the bottom corner shifted and tore the day of my parent's divorce. I believe her when she says it righted by itself a few days later without her praying or waiting for another miracle—auras trapped in chants and prayers. I believe in their colors and faces, the mix and hue I have never been shown, robes and brilliant flames branding the path of the folktale into a personal myth of reflection and rainbow worship, whose transformation across the texts of sinners can never be questioned.

I watch the old women pray to them because they have no choice and believe in the witnessing of the act—a lesson for the child who colored the cross with the wrong crayon. I believe in staring at the walls of my grandmother's apartment because hypnotism lies inside the calendars, between the bibles and rosary boxes. They will move the day the old women die, leave their pictures for me to fold and take away because there is a torn face of an unnamed saint slowly emerging through the ink stains left behind the photos stuck on walls for ninety years.

◆

A stone bridge
crosses the top
of the arroyo

where a man lives
waters his wisdom
plants the ground
with harmony
and red eyes

A stone bridge
crosses the top
of the arroyo

where a man lives
sleeps his owl
until it awakes
with an egg
clutched in its claws

◆

A morning with people on the way to the story.
A gleam in their eyes.
The rain has stopped.
Fresh smells of the earth return them to their houses.

◆

The fields have hidden secrets among the rows of corn.
The fields have communities hidden among the cotton.
The fields have nests hidden among the grapes.

◆

The turtle is innocent.
Do not blame it for the loss.

The cries are guilty.
Mark them as villages.

Song puddles are the source.
They spawn the egg.

Tree houses are given.
They burn upon invasion.

What is left is decided.
What is left is myth.

◆

So what if his family originated as a bunch of ugly turtles with ugly heads
and awful claws and the slowness of history had to do with mud and hiding
and swimming and spawning and feeding and dying and floating and painting
dreams on hard shells to teach the others this was the only direction the river
allowed before it dried up and kissed sand?

◆

In the grief of broken eggs,
men depart and leave families.
In the grief of forested hours,
men come back and fight.
In the grief of desert and sea,
men walk and stare at their feet.

◆

Man Walking across the White Sands National Monument

Everything in the world belongs to him.
The black tower has stood for fifty years,
the fenced-off area holding the invisible silhouette
of explosions within the encircled air,
hard pieces of ground untouched by his approach,
their chemicals dancing deep into the earth
as he comes closer.

He crosses the white sands to see where
they told him his bellybutton came from.
When he opened his eyes for the first time,
the umbilical cord led down to places below
the dunes he would never know.
He leaves footprints across the white sands,
destroys details about his life,
how the birth of his only son was preceded
by a black light that fell across his shoulder
the instant his wife screamed and pushed,

the light turning into a mole on his left arm,
reminding him of the moon he can't extract
from the corner of his right eyelid,
the white circle opening and closing each time
he finds the albino rattlesnake crawling
on the ground toward him,
lines it leaves across the smooth sand
the only marks left in the shattered world.

•

No host.
No tree.

No step into snow derived from memory as if stepping aside bends wisdom
   into the drum
of vibrating caskets where the people buried their beliefs.

No saying.
No legend that fits.

No story beside the white form of the river where one horse lost the other,
   followed it into
the smoke from fields of onions carrying their weight into the air.

This is majesty driven out of the mind.
This is the friend who talked to the doves, told them to be still.

This is the artist in the small of the back who aches for release.
This is the soap in the onion that washes the mouth.

No name.
No sin.

No communion wafer to dance around as if bread clears the body of hidden
   points
between veins, muscles, the growing cell of pure strength and belief.

No sound.
No cry.

No answer to the diminishing green branches of a changing soul who was
   worshipped as a
tongue lover who invented words made from the rain that gargled down the
   throats of
condemned men he prayed for.

◆

Broken Oval

He looked up toward heaven without knowing what he was looking for. He was told to look up, straining his neck to find something in the air that would not remind him about the self-imposed fissure on the ground. He didn't see anything, the few clouds in the sky drifting by his field of vision. He grew tired of squinting into the sun, closed his eyes, and looked down. In another version, he shows his son a broken oval he removed from his own ear years ago. It is a tiny green bone that bothered him, until he was able to feel it hanging. When he yanked it out, there was a little blood, but no pain. The broken oval has nothing to do with having to look up at the sky. It is mentioned because he was thinking about the time he showed his son the tiny bone he always kept in his shirt pocket. His son didn't say anything, thought his father was a strange man who loved to pick his ears, kept them dirty often, talking about skies with objects in them and how a man must slowly remove things from inside his head—to be a stronger man, a better father, someone who can lead his son to be involved in exceptions to rules. Why he thinks this, he doesn't know. His son does not want to talk to him very often. After glancing at the broken oval of bone his father held out to him, the boy shrugged and walked away. He didn't say anything to his father the rest of that day. Thinking back on it, he knows he never should have shown his son such an odd thing. Broken oval. Who would believe it came out of his head, the tiny object coming out of his ear as if it was nothing. Broken oval. What he never told his son.

♦

Jalapeño plant.
Two feet tall, green with white blossoms,
my jalapeño plant refuses to produce peppers.
I wait for the first jalapeño to appear on the striped stem,
wonder if I have done something wrong to keep the fire away,
the taste of the seed burning my tongue as if it has already happened.
I wait for my plant to give me my jalapeños,
let tears run down my face in practice for the bite,

the day I pull the pepper, offer it to the chili god
who pestered me with guilt and yearning,
the voice that told me the man who grows jalapeños
is the man whose tongue burned with the truth long ago.

•

You're in heaven now.
Your enemy is the flower left behind
by the doubt in the arc,
its cracked face distinguishing
the last sound of touch.

You're the answer at noon.
Your green blade is the vowel
caught in the throat of the woman
who carried the water,
made the men in her family
stand in a circle, hands outstretched,
waiting for a huge tortilla.
You see what hunger did.
The men took one bite from the warm tortilla,
passed it around the circle—
boys, uncles, fathers, strangers
who saw you leave them behind.

You're in heaven now.
Your bite was the largest one.
The tortilla was consumed without fish.
The woman with water got what she wanted,
no longer thinks about you day and night.
You're in possession now.
Even the mountain behind you
has stolen your face.

◆

He wakes to the shadow of the tarantula.
The form of the bleeding harp tingles in his ears.

He rises to a language of ecstasy,
knows he walked out of the black canyon with ease.

He steps into the shadow of the tarantula,
counts the seconds between color and his feet.

He has been seen as a dying bear,
claws raking the world for its ashes, its beliefs.

He goes to the fireplace and kneels,
the ashes gone into another taste.

He sees his hands will turn yellow when he digs
into the clay surrounding his house.

He forgets about the shadow of the tarantula.
It is going to make him stronger,

add length to his hair, force him
to close his eyes and come back

from a dance where he loved the women
who made him believe in himself.

He will no longer fear the things behind him,
nor have to look over his shoulder to find

the sunrise in the shadows is brimming
with water he drank when he was a child,

one or two tarantulas floating in the clay
to make sure he would never forget.

•

Driving south past Albuquerque through sixty miles of fog, the desert disappears behind white bodies of rolling clouds, murmurings of a time when we hid everything we knew behind the white faces of our nightmares, came up wet and breathing several miles down the road. Driving through fog that won't lift, I am lost in a place not visited in years, driving with headlights on, wondering if I will hit anything, turn the morning into a run between the fearful moon and the place everyone comes to when they can no longer see, no longer find the history of these pages to be the exact thing they want to say. Driving into blinding layers of white relics left quickly behind, I come into open sky and brake for a moment of relief, sorrow in the flesh of the cloud, the silence of knowing too many things are over and the amphibian tracks are in the world, not knowing where that world ends and my own begins, where the fog parts as distant red mountains quit their praying. Suddenly, I am inside the fog again, forget the exact moment I slam into something that has already happened pages ago. A brief image of an arroyo cuts past lesser animals I was warned about—a humming movement through this cloud where I once lived when I believed the highway home was pure exhaustion, each road a scar over my left shoulder.

•

Tonight above the hated river,
a peak is rising to change the sky
and give the blue horizon my life
through thought, desire, the moving body
that yearns for brilliant questions
to squeeze water out of the brain.

Brain into water into river minus the hate,
so I can cross barefoot and point my toes
toward the moon, laughing because it is
the same arrogance of the old man who rubbed
his feet with the killing cure of river alcohol.

Tonight below the sleeping song of the tumbleweed,
a hot breeze captures the path of dryness,
opens the rocks to let me through,
brushes me with weed dust and fiber
to protect the brown lines on my forehead.

◆

The Dark Brother

smoking paper cloth reappearing with the image of Christ burnt and woven
arms and legs—the dark brother comes up the stairs senses me turns resists
the Catholic miracle demands an answer to the sweat can't accept the scorched
sheet is family legacy each door a flight of the arrow each movement a prayer—
movement as prayer the stillness dancing to cure eyesight sharpen the need to
believe we are full of grace—if existence remains too long we are caught inside
its wishes—the forest inside the egg belongs to the man with no shame the
serenade in the gasping barrio the wailing of mourning mothers—no other
self but the man who threw rosaries away no feather to fall and cup into the
fear of hands tear into the tattoo that breathes on the chest—across the road
a lake a fire—yesterday the dark brother comes up the stairs wounded ceiling
for his polished shoes hidden room of shell treasures—embracing roping us
ravenous with strength thinking about blood calling responding with a letter to
a lost son not knowing why only to stay alive—collection of musicians unable
to speak English but they can play waiting for one more shot at the empti-
ness between hands—the dark brother comes up the stairs says to go home
no sense in magic no drunk curandero can be believed—no one here speaks of
miracles and lives no way mother and father will learn the language no way

we can interpret what was in their skulls the night they threw things at each
other gave birth to the idea of not having time to be poor—only time to dis-
integrate the family forever—tortuga history wrapped in a bed roll and cast
to the road—incense of sweat weight of sincerity left ajar basket with memo-
ries basket with moldy tortillas—the dark brother comes up the stairs finally
arrives says only so much counts the orphan the drummer remain the orphan
and his brother are the same.

◆

You don't know this temple,
this acquisition, its tempered crown
of love and asking—
a solemn object held to the breast
so you can see how many years have passed.
You don't know this temple,
how it arrives to cover you with invisible force
that allows you to prosper after
the cost has been paid.
You don't know this temple
and it is as simple as this:
Once, a torrid rain washed your face.

◆

The song came easy for some of us.

The song boys sang took me there.
I bowed down, admitted

mud on my hands
belonged to the first boy

who beat me
to the digging,

the one who wanted the song
only for himself, didn't know

it belonged to men who sang it
before the boys of hatred were born.

The song came easy for most of us,
but we were too busy being called

"spic, beaner, greaser, wetback."
So we sang that easy song first,

hummed the words like
our hunted fathers before us,

gave up on the sound men kneel for,
muddy hands digging for notes,

caves for shelter from stronger men,
the sound of hands using mud

to shape the easy song,
build the stronger wall.

◆

When he disappeared at the edge of the sky,
someone said he was a Chicano.

When he found seeds planted inside wounds,
someone said he could not spell.

When he traced the century's rooftop,
someone said it was his house all along.

When he laughed and shattered the apples,
someone gave him tortillas and eggs and all these stories.

When he plunged into twilight,
someone saw him in Mexico City retelling these things.

When he grew his hair green,
someone wrote a poem about him.

When he replaced joy with a hugging rhythm,
someone showed him the end of the road.

When he went there to eat adobe,
someone whispered it was already in his heart.

When he went upstairs to open a window,
someone was there waiting for him.

About the Author

Ray Gonzalez is a poet, essayist, and editor born in El Paso, Texas. He is the author of *Memory Fever* (The University of Arizona Press, 1999), a memoir about growing up in the Southwest, and five books of poetry, including *Cabato Sentora* (1999) and *The Heat of Arrivals* (1996), both from BOA Editions. The latter received a 1997 PEN/Oakland Josephine Miles Book Award for Excellence in Literature.

He is the editor of twelve anthologies, most recently *Muy Macho: Latino Men Confront Their Manhood* and *Touching the Fire: Fifteen Poets of the Latino Renaissance*, both from Anchor/Doubleday Books. He has served as Poetry Editor for *The Bloomsbury Review* for seventeen years and recently founded a new poetry journal, *LUNA*.

His awards include a 1998 Fellowship in Poetry from The Illinois Arts Council, a 1993 Before Columbus Foundation American Book Award for Excellence in Editing, and a 1988 Colorado Governor's Award for Excellence in the Arts. He formerly taught at the University of Illinois at Chicago and now holds an endowed chair, the McKnight Land Grant Professorship, at the University of Minnesota in Minneapolis.

Works by Ray Gonzalez

Essays and Memoirs

Memory Fever: A Journey Beyond El Paso del Norte
Turtle Pictures

Poetry

Apprentice to Volcanos
Cabato Sentora
From the Restless Roots
The Heat of Arrivals
Railroad Face
Twilights and Chants

Anthologies

After Aztlan: Latino Poets of the Nineties
City Kite on a Wire: 38 Denver Poets
Crossing the River: Poets of the Western U.S.

Currents from the Dancing River: Contemporary Latino Fiction, Nonfiction, and Poetry

Inheritance of Light

The Midnight Lamp

Mirrors Beneath the Earth: Short Fiction by Chicano Writers

Muy Macho: Latino Men Confront Their Manhood

Touching the Fire: Fifteen Poets of Today's Latino Renaissance

Under the Pomegranate Tree: The Best New Latino Erotica

Without Discovery: A Native Response to Columbus

Journals

The Guadalupe Review

LUNA: A New Journal of Poetry